Thomas Lamb Phipson

Famous violinists and fine violins

Historical notes, anecdotes and reminiscences

Thomas Lamb Phipson

Famous violinists and fine violins
Historical notes, anecdotes and reminiscences

ISBN/EAN: 9783337204389

Printed in Europe, USA, Canada, Australia, Japan

Cover: Foto ©Thomas Meinert / pixelio.de

More available books at **www.hansebooks.com**

Famous Violinists and Fine Violins

Historical Notes, Anecdotes, and Reminiscences

By

Dr. T. L. Phipson

Formerly President and Violin Solo to the
Bohemian Orchestral Society

Author of
"Scenes from the Reign of Louis XVI.," etc.

London
Chatto & Windus, Piccadilly
Philadelphia: J. B. Lippincott Company
1896

Dedication

TO

SIGNOR GUIDO PAPINI

Hon. President of the College of Violinists

The high reputation which your compositions for the violin have obtained in this country, and, indeed, in every quarter of the civilised world, induces me to dedicate to you the following pages.

That the name of so celebrated a musician should adorn this modest little volume is perhaps more than it deserves, since you are the direct descendant of the immortal Corelli, Tartini, and Viotti, and, like them, have caused the beneficent influence of Italian music to spread around the globe for the delight and welfare of mankind. But I take advantage of our long and affectionate friendship to inscribe here a name so universally beloved and admired.

THE AUTHOR.

PREFACE

MUSIC began for me in what may well be termed a paradise on earth; and often have I thanked Providence that, by its means, the joys of this world have almost equalled the sorrows which, alas! are inseparable from our existence. A lovely country in Warwickshire, not far from the home of Shakespeare, a splendid mansion, with beautiful gardens and meadows, stabling for six horses, ponds, and woods of majestic elms and beeches, made up an abode such as can only be found in Merry England. It is natural enough that an intense love of melody should have entered my childish heart with the song of the wild birds and the perfumes of the flowers. There was music constantly in our house at Ladywood, and all around us.

When my father returned from the University of Jena, where he had passed a good many years, he brought back with him, not only a fine collection of student songs, but a violin. He was taught the violin during his residence in Germany; and though I never heard him play more than a few notes, I have ample proof that he was one of the best judges of good playing that ever lived; and he would not allow the slightest bad taste or false note to be produced in his presence without correcting it at once.

My first violin came to me under rather peculiar circumstances, when I was not quite six years of age. I had been very ill with scarlet fever, but had recovered wonderfully since my mother had allowed me to sponge my aching head over a bucket of cold water. One morning my father entered my bedroom; he said he was going to ride into Birmingham, and asked me what he should bring back for me to play with. Without a moment's hesitation I exclaimed, "A violin!"

Why did I say that? Why did I ask for an instrument which was destined ever afterwards to cling to me through life, to soothe my sorrows, to become a source of delight, and to lead me through endless adventures? Heaven alone knows! I asked for a violin, and my good father, to my great joy, actually brought one to me. It was cautiously wrapped, with its bow, and a little box of rosin, in a brown paper parcel, so that he could carry it attached to the pommel of his saddle. To describe the feeling of contentment and the enthusiasm with which I opened this precious parcel, as I sat up in bed exulting over my good fortune, would be quite impossible. But, alas! when it was opened I could do nothing but silently admire the contents.

There was, sure enough, a magnificent violin, with a brilliant golden varnish which would have shamed Joseph Guarnerius *filius Andreæ* himself. The strings were perfectly new and clean, and the bow, of a lovely crimson colour, with its white hair and ivory nut, appeared splendid. According to my father's instructions, the bow was passed several times over the rosin before being drawn across the strings, and when at last this operation was performed, there issued from the instrument, which had been carefully tuned, the most extraordinary sound; it was something between that of an Eolian harp and the buzzing of a bumble-bee.

It pleased me exceedingly, and I was delighted at the ease with which it was produced; but, at the same time, a feeling of powerlessness came over me as the sounds on the open strings were repeated several times, and the want of variety took possession of my mind. It was like the music of some composers I could name—mostly *fifths*, and decidedly monotonous.

My excellent father grasped the situation at once, and showing me how to hold the instrument properly, he placed my fingers on the finger-board, pressing them down and pulling them up alternately, whilst I drew the bow across the strings, and caused it to scrape out a simple little melody.

That was my first lesson on the violin.

In a few days, sitting up in bed, and grasping the

instrument firmly, I could play this little air with tolerable satisfaction to myself, whatever it might have been to others; and when a few months had elapsed I had made what is generally termed "considerable progress." But yet I had only this little melody of eight bars. It was pretty, it was easy, and it was so simple that it really required no accompaniment. At this juncture a friend, who was a violinist, happened to call at our house, and whilst in the corridor he heard the sound of my music upstairs. Turning to my parents, he said, "If your child is going to learn music, you should have him taught the violin, for he has got something, naturally, which we violinists have to work for, sometimes for years."

However, my mother had decided upon having me taught the piano by a lady from the Royal Academy of Music, whom she was befriending at that time. The piano lessons went very well so long as the right hand only was engaged; but when it came to studying the bass clef, and using the left hand at the same time as the right, it proved too much for my feelings; and I hugged my violin with more tenderness than ever. I did more; I ran out into the open country, far across the flowery meadows, whenever the hour of the piano lesson approached, and stayed there till it was too late and the music mistress had gone! This convinced my dear parents that the piano was of no use; so, when about six years of age, a violin master was engaged for me.

In those days we lived in England under the fascinating influence of the beautiful, melodious Italian Opera. My father was a friend of the celebrated Malibran (afterwards the wife of De Bériot), and many members of my family, when in London, went night after night to hear her. I remember, also, being taken to hear Madame Castellan, in *Norma* and *La Sonnambula*, a few years later. My music master was a member of the orchestra of the Italian Opera; but he had retired and opened a music shop in Birmingham. His name was Allwood. He was also a good enough pianist to play accompaniments for his pupils, and under his clever guidance I was taught to sing on the violin. After the preliminary drudgery, which he abridged as much as possible, he placed before me the most luscious melodies of the Italian masters, supporting them with his piano part, which kept the violin perfectly in tune, whilst the rising and falling of the accompaniment helped to induce the proper expression.

It appears that the music shop did not answer. Poor Allwood had to return to the orchestra in London, and I thus lost his valuable instruction.

There passed through our part of the country at this time a fine Hungarian orchestra which created some sensation. The leader was a brilliant violinist;

my father made his acquaintance, and I had a few lessons from him. Every time he came he took a sheet of paper and wrote out the exercise he desired me to play—he was very fond of the key of A minor—but he could not speak a word of English, which made it rather awkward, as I knew very few words of German then.

Soon, however, I was destined to quit this beautiful and blissful abode, and, like that Hungarian violinist, go across the sea to foreign lands, taking with me Spohr's "Violin School," and a few little Italian pieces which my mother accompanied beautifully on the piano.

In Brussels I had three lessons a week, for five years, from Henri Standish, the able *répétiteur* of the class of De Bériot at the Conservatoire de Musique; and I attended the Italian and French operas very frequently. In 1856 I left for Paris, where I had many musical friends, and where I joined an orchestra for a short time. But science and literature claimed most of my time there. During the last thirty years or so that I have resided almost constantly in my own country, my violin has been in very frequent requisition. My *répertoire*, which has served me in hundreds of public concerts and *soirées musicales*, comprises the compositions of De Bériot, Paganini, Panofka, Hauser, Lafont, Artot, Dancla, Bazzini, Alard, Ernst, Papini, and several other less known composers. For four years I

PREFACE

acted as leader and violin solo to the Bohemian Orchestral Society in London, which gave many brilliant concerts.

It is not surprising that, with so much musical work, and a natural fondness for history, I should have become more and more interested in everything connected with my instrument, and with those whom it has brought into celebrity. Most people will admit that music is not only one of our greatest enjoyments, but that it is almost essential to the welfare of mankind, tending, as it does, to encourage us in the pursuit of all that is fine and beautiful. It was under this impression that, many years ago, I wrote my "Biographical Sketches of Celebrated Violinists," a work that was very well received; and it is with the same feelings that I am now induced to bring out the present volume, which I trust will be found more useful, and, perhaps, not less interesting.

CASA MIA, PUTNEY,
June 1896.

CONTENTS

CHAP.		PAGE
I.	THE GREAT VIOLINISTS OF THE ITALIAN SCHOOL	1
II.	THE LEADER OF THE ROYAL VIOLINS	32
III.	CHERUBINI AS A VIOLINIST	38
IV.	THE SECRET OF PAGANINI	44
V.	THE VIOLIN DAYS OF BALFE	64
VI.	CHARLES AUGUSTE DE BÉRIOT (1802–1870)	73
VII.	A SOUVENIR OF SIVORI	90
VIII.	THE TWO JOSEPHS OF CREMONA	97
IX.	A VIOLIN RECITAL IN MONGOLIA	110
X.	VIOLINS OF VALUE	117
XI.	THE STRADIUARIUS—A DIALOGUE	124
XII.	OLAUS BULL AND NORWEGIAN POETRY	130
XIII.	THE CHILD VIOLINIST	150
XIV.	THE ORCHESTRA AND THE SINGER	170
XV.	SECRETS OF THE "CREMONA VIOLIN" TRADE	175

CONTENTS

CHAP.		PAGE
XVI.	THE VIOLIN SCHOOL AT NEUILLY	184
XVII.	THE "SOUL" OF THE VIOLIN, OR THE SECRET OF THE SOUND-POST	221
XVIII.	THE BRIDGE, THE STRINGS, AND THE BOW	233
XIX.	PERSONAL RECOLLECTIONS OF HENRI VIEUXTEMPS	240

INDEX 249

Famous Violinists

I

THE GREAT VIOLINISTS OF THE ITALIAN SCHOOL

ITALY is the classic soil of the violin. To Italy we must look for the greatest of violin-players and for the finest makers of the instrument.

Indeed, whether we take into consideration instrumental music, singing, painting, sculpture, or architecture, we find in Italy a constant source of power and beauty which has in ages past spread its beneficent influence over the whole of the civilised world. To no other country do we owe such an enormous debt of melody and inspiration.

As the French writer Choron says, "the Italians have been the instructors of all Europe in instrumental composition," to which we may safely add, "and in many other things."

In violin music the compositions of the Italian masters have been made the models from which all other solo pieces have been constructed. Modern

Italian music is no longer quite the same thing. It has deviated considerably from the fine old paths so well trodden by Tartini, Viotti, Campagnoli, Rossini, and other celebrated composers. It now bears the impress of French and German influence, and has deteriorated accordingly. Though it is still replete with good taste and delicacy, it has lost a great amount of its former dramatic power. Some of the compositions of Tosti and Papini, for instance, are exquisitely beautiful, but in many we can trace the influence of Charles Gounod. In his later productions even the veteran Verdi is said to have given strong evidence of having felt the effects of the music of Richard Wagner. This is exceedingly curious when we recollect that the principal strain of the celebrated "March" in *Tannhauser* is almost note for note the fine air sung by Manrico in Verdi's *Trovatore*, which came out a few years before the first-named opera.

The very first violinist of eminence was an Italian, a musician named Battista, or Giovanni Battista, to whom some old writers allude about the year 1590 as being a very clever performer. At the latter end of the sixteenth century, however, the violin was yet little known and appreciated, though both Italy and France could boast of some charming players upon the *viola d'amore*, a much larger instrument, which may yet make its appearance again in our drawing-rooms.

THE ITALIAN SCHOOL 3

About the middle of the seventeenth century a musical ecclesiastic, Padre Castrovillari, of Padua, became eminent both as a violinist and composer. He left a pupil, named Bassani, who wrote several compositions for the church and the theatre, and who became the teacher of the celebrated Corelli.

In 1769 Bassani published several sonatas, and was well known as a distinguished performer on the violin. His pupil Corelli, who had had some lessons previously from Matteo Simonelli in religious music, afterwards became famous, and instructed (among other men who have left names in the musical world) an eccentric writer for the violin named Locatelli, whose studies are thought to have helped Paganini in perfecting his extraordinary talent. He certainly appears to have discovered some curious "harmonic" and other effects, which are not of very great importance, and of which his sober classical teacher had evidently no notion.

At the period during which the celebrated violin-makers of the Tyrol and Cremona were supplying violinists and bass-players with instruments which for combined sweetness and power are now classed among the wonders of the world, three eminent names tower above the horizon of distinguished *virtuosi* —Corelli, Tartini, and Viotti—to whose splendid methods are due almost all that is achieved at the present day in the art of violin-playing, and whose united careers extend over a space of about 150 years.

We must not, however, attach too great a significance to the term "school," since Paganini and Tartini were independent of any, and, like Shakespeare and Molière, belonged to no academy. Nevertheless, Paganini himself would probably never have played the violin at all, but have contented himself with his father's mandoline, had there been no such men as Corelli and Tartini to lay down the principles of broad style and good taste.

It was in the month of February 1653 that a child was born at Fusignano, in the territory of Bologna, whose career was destined to exert an immense influence in the musical world, and particularly in the art of violin-playing. The name of this child was Archangelo Corelli. His compositions have come down to us as types of purity and freshness, and his tomb in the Pantheon at Rome, near to that of Raffaele, bears the inscription : *Corelli princeps musicorum.*

Corelli's life, like that of most musicians, was one of numerous adventures and mishaps; nevertheless he has left a great name. To show how little affinity existed between Italian and German music even in those early days, it is related on excellent authority that Corelli once had to lead one of Handel's compositions, in which the Italian violinist gave to the opening movement a style of his own. Handel, who had studied the violin to some extent, lost his temper, as usual on such occasions, and so

THE ITALIAN SCHOOL 5

far forgot himself as to snatch the instrument from the hand of Corelli, to show him where the accent fell. The latter replied, with his accustomed mildness, " My dear Saxon, this music is in the foreign style, which I do not understand at all." A much more serious mishap occurred to Corelli at Naples, where he was astonished at the brilliant playing of the orchestra. Out of compliment to his great reputation, he was appointed to lead a composition by Scarlatti ; and on arriving at an air in A minor, he led off in C major. We are told by rival contemporaries that it was some considerable time before he could discern his mistake ; but that is palpably absurd.

As the result of assiduous labour Corelli became a great violinist, his fame spreading far and wide, and the number of his pupils increasing year by year. He was appointed leader of the orchestra at Rome about the year 1690. As a solo player, we are assured, his style was learned and elegant, his tone firm and even, and his performance occasionally impressed with feeling. No doubt it was somewhat cold—the usual result of too much labour—and when, several years later, he played before the King of Naples, that monarch was so wearied with one of Corelli's adagios that he got up and left the room before the piece was finished. Again, at Cardinal Ottoboni's in Rome, his patron and protector, the playing of Corelli was not striking enough to cause the company to cease talking during his performance. This circumstance so annoyed the great *virtuoso* that he stopped playing and stepped down from the platform, saying, in his calm, good-natured manner, that he was afraid the "noise of his music might interfere with the conversation."

A man of a very different stamp was Giuseppe Tartini, born in 1692, a gentleman by birth and education, who at the early age of twenty-two, whilst still prosecuting his studies at the University of Padua, composed his immortal *Sonata del Diavolo*, now usually called *Il Trillo del Diavolo*. He was originally intended for the law, but circumstances led him to adopt music as a profession. As a youth he was extremely fond of music and fencing—few could match him with the foils. He began to study the violin seriously under Giulio di Terni, a clever musician, who, in after years, came and took some lessons from his celebrated pupil. An early marriage, contracted against the consent of his parents, caused the young man to fly and seek a livelihood far from the parental eyes. A relative, who was an abbot at the monastery of Assisi, befriended him, and he laboured in that secluded spot to perfect his violin-playing, taking part regularly in the religious music of the establishment. After reconciliation with his family he went to Venice, in order that he might hear the eccentric

THE ITALIAN SCHOOL 7

Veracini, the *capo pazzo*, or madcap; a violinist whose performances produced so great an effect upon him that it was this said Veracini whom he saw in his dream, or nightmare, on awaking from which he composed his clever *Sonata del Diavolo*, a piece in which a series of double-shakes, and the satanic laugh with which it concludes, are so dear to lovers of descriptive music.

This composition, strange to relate, actually helped him to the appointment of director of the orchestra in the Church of St. Anthony at Padua in 1721; and by the year 1728 he had founded a great violin school in that celebrated old city. Another of his compositions, *Didone Abandonata* (Sonata X.), is quite as descriptive.

Before he died (February 1770) Tartini had perfected the art of bowing, had composed eighteen Concertos for five instruments, as well as several Trios and a number of Sonatas, and left a *Tratto di Musica*, or treatise on music, in which he discusses the curious acoustic phenomenon known as "the third sound," *i.e.*, the production of a third note in harmony when only two notes are struck with the bow.

*Viotti combined the talents of Corelli and Tartini. Like the latter, he was a man of poetic and philosophic mind. His birth occurred at the little village of Fontaneto, in Piedmont, in 1755. How he took to violin-playing as a profession nobody seems to know. He was a pupil of the celebrated Pugnani, of Turin, at the age of twenty, a wine merchant in London at forty-seven, leader of the Grand Opera in Paris at sixty-six, and died in London (or Brighton?) 24th March 1824, at the age of sixty-nine.

His zenith of fame was just before the time of Paganini and De Bériot, and no performer had ever attained so high a degree of perfection, so fine a tone, such sustained elegance, such dramatic power, and so varied a style. Beauty and grandeur were the characteristics of his playing.

Viotti shone in society as well as in the concert room. The latter he abandoned very early in his career, jealous of the applause bestowed upon others whom he knew to be inferior to himself. He played with great success in London in 1790, at which period his *compatriote*, the celebrated *prima donna*, Brigitta Banti, was still singing at the Opera here; and he was leader of the orchestra at the King's Theatre about 1794, but soon afterwards retired to Holland—it is generally supposed for certain political reasons—where, in perfect seclusion, he wrote his well-known *Six Duets* for two violins, and other esteemed compositions. I have said elsewhere that in this justly celebrated man we find the link which connects the modern school of violin-playing with the schools of the past; and though he had during the whole of his career only

THE ITALIAN SCHOOL 9

seven or eight pupils, yet his influence has extended throughout the world, and is felt by composers of the present day, even after the wonderful flights of Paganini, De Bériot, and Ernst.

Viotti was universally regarded as the greatest violinist of his time, though he must have been run very closely by his contemporary Campagnoli, of Dresden, and several others. He was one of those rare phenomena in the world of art in whom talent and modesty were admirably combined, and in whom the powers of the *virtuoso* were equalled by those of the composer.

After being appointed, at twenty years of age, first violin to the Chapel Royal at Turin, a position which he held for three years, he travelled for some time as a solo player. Meeting with a most flattering reception at Berlin, he continued his course to Paris, where he arrived when he was about twenty-five years of age, and made his first appearance at the *Concerts Spirituels*, the chief place at that time where artistes of eminence were introduced to the Parisian public.

The *Concerts Spirituels* were established in March 1725, as a kind of annex to the Opera, like the Promenade Concerts of our time in London. They were given in one of the rooms in the Palace of the Tuileries, and were continued until the outbreak of the Revolution. Their name is due to the fact that they were devoted chiefly to sacred music, or to music of a serious character, for some considerable time after their foundation.

Viotti's *début* at these concerts was extremely successful; no violinist had yet been heard there who possessed so fine a tone and so large a style. He performed several of his own compositions, Concertos, which were decidedly superior to the works of the same kind previously heard in Paris.

When we reflect on the considerable number of eminent violinists in that city at the period of which I am writing, it is very evident that the young Giovanni Battista Viotti must have possessed extraordinary talent to have eclipsed them all. Indeed, he had not been long in the French capital, where he was destined to reside for so many years, before he attracted attention in the highest quarters; he soon received the command of Queen Marie Antoinette to play at the Court of Versailles.

It was on one of these occasions that a characteristic scene occurred, illustrating the peculiarly courageous nature of Viotti, which was to be found not only in his playing and in his compositions, but likewise in his private life. The concert had been most carefully arranged, and our *virtuoso* had just commenced one of his charming Concertos when the arrogant Count d'Artois, a most conceited fop, entered the room, and made a great noise, walking about and speaking in a loud voice to

THE ITALIAN SCHOOL 11

several persons of his acquaintance among the numerous and brilliant company assembled. All this bustle interrupted the music, and the performance suffered accordingly. At first Viotti controlled his feelings, and gave way to the annoyance; a little silence ensuing, he began his piece again. But the same uproar recommencing soon afterwards, he was seen to throw a scornful glance at the unmannerly Count, and at once withdrew from the concert room without further ceremony.

This scene at Versailles seems to have had a serious effect upon Viotti's ultimate career; for ever afterwards he evinced the greatest dislike to appear in public as a solo-player. Once only he played for a charity, and once again in 1790, at a singular concert given by a member of the Revolutionary Government, who was a friend of his, when the audience, among whom were many members of the unfortunate aristocracy, were compelled to mount three or four flights of stairs, and found that the only decoration in the room was a bust of Jean Jacques Rousseau!

In private circles Viotti was often the charm of the evening. He played in several drawing-rooms, where his friend Garat, the favourite tenor singer, was often heard, and also the young Orfila, a Portuguese medical student, who became later in life distinguished as the author of an important treatise on the detection of "Poisons," a noted chemist and toxicologist, but at that time frequently enchanted his hearers by his exquisite voice.

When Viotti had abandoned the concert room, one of his greatest delights was to improvise violin parts to the piano-playing of his friend, Madame Montegerault, at her house in the suburb of Montmorency. This amiable and talented lady would seat herself at the piano and play a brilliant improvisation in the Concerto style, and Viotti would take up his violin and join in the performance, producing a series of extempore passages which admirably displayed his wonderful powers and delighted all present.

With all this, he did not keep clear of meddling in the disturbed politics of the period—or, perhaps, they meddled with him—and he was compelled to fly from Paris, as did his friend Cherubini, who had resided with him for about three years, and in 1792 he came suddenly to London; Cherubini meanwhile seeking refuge at a friend's house near Rouen. Both these eminent musicians were at that time engaged at the *Théâtre Feydeau*, and all the artistes of that opera house fled likewise to escape the horrors of the Revolution.

In London Viotti appeared at the well-known Salomon's Concerts. Every one was charmed with his originality, his fine large bowing, bold style, and refined taste. But his dislike to performing at concerts as a solo-player, and his speculative

THE ITALIAN SCHOOL

turn of mind, induced him to take a share in the management of the King's Theatre about the years 1794-95, and he became leader of the orchestra there.

It was during this period, we are assured, that Viotti received "an order from the British Government" to quit England at once! Certainly that seems rather curious. The authenticity of that order, or its reason, I have never been able to discover. Some writers suppose it to have been connected with political matters, but it seems very much more reasonable to suppose that the celebrated violinist found that the management of the King's Theatre was running him into debt, and that he was really obliged to fly from his creditors. In fact, the "order from the British Government" may have been something in the nature of a writ!

Anyhow, he went over to a secluded spot in Holland, to a place called Schonfeld, where he wrote several of his best compositions; and in the course of a few years, when his troubles, whatever they may have been, had subsided, he returned to England.

This was in 1801, and, however strange and incredible it may appear, he came to London this time to establish himself as a wine merchant. We find him now at the head of a considerable concern, surrounded by clerks and customers, attending punctually to business during the day, and charming his friends with his violin in the evening.

In this manner Viotti's taste for speculation utterly ruined him; it was not very long before he lost everything in this extraordinary undertaking by which he hoped, no doubt, to realise a fortune much more rapidly than by his violin. It is generally admitted that military men and musicians often make bad men of business. The tenor Garat, who came over to London about this time, has described a dinner-party given by Viotti after the commercial labours of the day had terminated. In the evening there was music. A young lady sang some beautiful songs by Cimarosa, and Viotti played one of his Concertos. "Never," says Garat, "was his bow more gifted or more sublime."

It is not my object to give a dry, critical analysis of the writings of this great violinist, but those of my readers who may happen to be unacquainted with his compositions should look at his celebrated *Six Duets* and at some of his *Concertos*.[1] They will soon perceive that the influence of Corelli in these works comes out more clearly than that of Tartini; the latter being, like Paganini and De Bériot, to a great extent an outsider—that is, an original genius who created his own style, and did not implicitly follow the lines of any "school."

---

[1] Ch. Dancla edited twelve of the finest (printed by Chalot, Paris), with the fingering and annotations.

THE ITALIAN SCHOOL 15

Viotti is a creative genius so far as he improved considerably in boldness on the style of Corelli. An excellent example of his work is the *Rondo Appassionata*, which is to be found arranged as a duet for two violins, with piano accompaniment by Papini, in the clever "Album Chanot," or "Soirée Concertante d'Amateurs Virtuoses," recently published in London by F. W. Chanot. On the cover of this interesting publication, which contains a number of fine pieces, is a picture of two ladies and a gentleman performing this effective little piece of Viotti before a very distinguished audience. Among the *Concertos*, that in D is extremely brilliant. The theme is taken from a trio in E flat by his celebrated teacher, Pugnani, of Turin.

Whilst Viotti held the post of director of the music at the Grand Opera in Paris, he received a letter from a man destined to take, in later years, the very foremost rank as a composer. I allude to Rossini. This letter is dated 10th July 1821, at which period Viotti was a greater man than Rossini. Here is my translation of it :—

"MOST ESTEEMED SIR,—You will be surprised at receiving a letter from an individual who has not the honour of your personal acquaintance, but I profit by the liberality of feeling existing between artistes to address these lines to you through our friend Hérold, from whom I have learned with the greatest satisfaction the high, and I fear somewhat undeserved, opinion you have of me. The oratorio of *Moise*, composed by me three years ago, appears to our mutual friend susceptible of dramatic adaptation to French words; and I who have the greatest reliance on Hérold's taste and on his friendship for me, desire nothing more than to render the entire work as perfect as possible, by composing new airs in a more religious style than those which it at present contains, and endeavouring to the full extent of my power that the result shall neither disgrace the composer of the partition, nor you, its patron and protector. If Signor Viotti, with his great ability, will consent to be the Mecænas of my name, he may be assured of the gratitude of his devoted servant.

    (Signed) "GIOACCHINO ROSSINI.

"*P.S.*—In a month's time I will forward to you the alterations of the drama *Moise*, in order that you may judge if they are conformable to the operatic style. Should they not be so, you will have the kindness to suggest any others better adapted to the purpose."

Here we have the great Rossini seeking advice and patronage from Viotti, and feeling his way to the Grand Opera of Paris, where, a few years later, his immortal *Guillaume Tell* caused such thunders

THE ITALIAN SCHOOL 17

of applause, and ensured for the composer a reputation which has never been eclipsed.

The greatest of all Viotti's pupils was probably Pierre Rode, whose well-known *Air Varié* and *Seventh Concerto* are familiar to most violinists who have had to go through the regular routine.

Besides this eminent man, this emblem of purity and neatness of execution, Viotti instructed the Belgian artiste Robbrechts, from whom De Bériot had lessons; and among his other pupils may be named Libon, Cartier, Labarre, Aldoy, Pixis, Mori, Vacher, Mdlle. Gerbini, and Madame Paravicini.

When De Bériot went to Paris and applied for advice and instruction to Viotti, the latter told him that he had already an original style which only required cultivating to lead to success, and that he could do nothing for him. The great Italian violinist felt, no doubt, that Charles De Bériot, one of the most gifted composers for his instrument that ever lived, had already achieved a step in advance, and that to go back to the more rigidly classical forms could only be done at the expense of the originality and power which ultimately raised De Bériot to the very highest rank as a soloist, a composer, and a teacher.

Among the pupils of Viotti, the celebrated Rode was not able to remain in Paris as he desired; he returned to his native place, Bordeaux, where he died at the age of fifty-seven, after a life of many

B

griefs, disappointments, and troubles. Labarre is said to have been a splendid soloist, especially in adagio movements, into which, like Viotti his master, he was accustomed to introduce ornamental inspirations. Libon, we are told, played with much sweetness, and was fine upon the fourth string. Mdlle. Gerbini had a fine tone, but lacked warmth of expression; and Cartier was a distinguished theoretician and teacher. Mori became well known in London as an excellent artiste, but cold. It is related of him that when he told De Bériot he could do nothing with his *Airs Variés*, the latter simply replied, "They require to be played with expression." It was this same Mori who offered his violin and bow "for *eighteenpence*" after hearing Paganini at his first concert in London.

Regarding his dislike to play solos in public, Viotti seems to have discovered that mediocre talent often meets with as much applause as that of the greatest artistes. He once said to some of his pupils, "My young friends, artistes spoil the public, and the public spoils them."

It is well known that Corelli, Tartini, and Viotti never made a public display of execution or difficulties. Whilst Paganini sometimes realised as much as £600 (15,000 francs) in *one evening*, the immortal Viotti never received from M. Le Gros, the organiser of the Concerts in Paris from 1782 to 1784, more than 1200 francs (or £48) for *a whole*

THE ITALIAN SCHOOL 19

season, or about £4 or £5 for each concert. The violinist Mestrino got about the same, and Gervais about £3.

After leaving his position at the Grand Opera, Viotti retired on a small pension and came to England, where he died on the 24th March 1824. Some time ago I received a letter from the well-known violinist, Victor Buziau, inquiring whether I could inform him where Viotti was interred. Not only was I unable to give him the desired information, but since then it has been impossible to make any researches with the view of discovering his last resting-place. Alas! many a man of talent, like Mozart himself, sleeps in an unknown tomb!

Persons who knew Viotti intimately have left records of his highly poetical nature, and the value he attached to the simplest gifts of Providence. A modest violet discovered hidden among the leaves would transport him with joy. "All nature spoke to his heart," says M. Eymar, "and he yielded at once to its emotions."

As a man of business, we are told, the strictest integrity and honour regulated his transactions, and his feelings were kind and benevolent; whilst as a musician, he is said never to have been surpassed in any of the highest qualities of violin-playing.

During a visit to Switzerland he heard for the

first time the plaintive sound of a mountain horn, breathing forth the few notes of a *Ranz des Vaches*. This so struck him that he noted it down and sent it in a letter to one of his friends. We fortunately possess that letter; it runs as follows :—

"The *Ranz des Vaches* which I send you is neither that which our friend Jean Jacques [Rousseau] has presented to us, nor that of which M. de la Bord speaks in his work on Music. I cannot say whether it is known or not; all I know is that I heard it in Switzerland, and shall never forget it. Towards the decline of day I was sauntering along in one of those sequestered spots where flowers, verdure, streamlets, all united to form a picture of perfect harmony. There, without being fatigued, I seated myself on a fragment of rock and fell into a deep reverie. . . . Sounds broke on my ear which were sometimes of a hurried, sometimes of a prolonged and sustained character. I found that they proceeded from a mountain horn, and their effect was heightened by the tones of a plaintive female voice. I started from my daydreams, listened with breathless attention, and learned, or rather engraved upon my memory the *Ranz des Vaches* which I send you. In order to understand all its beauties, you ought to be transported to the scene in which I heard it, and to feel all the enthusiasm that such a moment inspired."

I can well appreciate Viotti's feelings on this

THE ITALIAN SCHOOL 21

occasion, for during a fine summer afternoon in June I also had the good fortune to pass a moment such as that so vividly described by the great violinist. It was among the German hills of Waldeck, whilst resting on a sunny slope, I heard for the first time in my life the tinkling of the distant sheep-bells coming from the side of a neighbouring hill, and gradually approaching the spot at which I sat listening to those fairy-like sounds. Nothing I have ever met with in music can completely realise the enchanting effect those soft, delicious sounds produced upon me, not even those charming mountain strains in Rossini's *Guillaume Tell*, nor Alard's beautiful little work *Souvenirs des Pyrénées*, not to speak of several clever pastoral piano solos, though there is something in all these that approaches the magical result to which I allude. This effect is, no doubt, heightened by the beauty of the surrounding scenery, the colours of the flowers, the fragrance of the air, the warm sunshine, and the thousand varied aspects of nature.

A very different kind of sound struck the ears of the celebrated Viotti when strolling one evening in Paris, on the Champs Elysées, with his friend Marie Langlé (father of the musician Ferdinand Langlé), by whom the circumstance is related. Marie Langlé was an excellent professor of harmony, a composer of some operatic works, and one of the instructors of the young military amateur, Lieutenant Dalayrac, who afterwards became a well-known composer and a great favourite with the French public.

It was a fine summer evening, night was approaching gradually, and the two friends had seated themselves on one of the benches under the trees to avoid the dust of the thoroughfare. Viotti, always of a dreamy, thoughtful disposition, had yielded to one of those reveries which isolated him even in the midst of a numerous and brilliant society, whilst Langlé sat thinking over some of the airs in his new opera *Corisandre*.

Suddenly they were both roused from their meditations by some harsh, discordant sounds, so terribly false that the two musicians, with astonishment depicted on their countenances, turned towards each other an inquiring glance, as much as to say, "What on earth is that?"

Viotti was the first to speak. "It can't be a violin!" he exclaimed; "and yet there is some resemblance."

"Nor a clarionet," suggested Langlé, "though it is something like one."

The easiest manner of solving the problem was to go and see. They approached the spot whence the extraordinary tones issued, and saw a poor blind man standing near a miserable candle, and playing upon a violin; but the instrument was made of tin-plate, like a coffee-pot.

"Fancy!" said Viotti, "it *is* a violin—but a tin violin! Did you ever dream of such a curiosity?"

And after listening for a few minutes he added—

"My dear Langlé, I must possess that instrument; go and ask the old man what he will take for it."

His companion approached and asked the question, but the old man was disinclined to part with it.

"We will give you enough to enable you to purchase a better violin," said Langlé; "and, pray, why is your instrument not like others?"

The aged musician explained that when he got old and found himself still poor, not being able to work, but yet able to scrape a few airs upon a fiddle, he had endeavoured to procure one, but in vain. At last his good, kind nephew, Eustache, who was apprenticed to a tinker, had made one for him in tin-plate.

"And a very good one, too!" said the old man. "My poor boy Eustache brings me here in the morning when he goes to work, and fetches me away in the evening as he returns."

"Well," said Viotti, "I will give you twenty francs for your instrument; you can buy a much better one for that price. But will you let me try it a little?"

The curious violin was placed in his hands. Its singular tone amused him, and he produced some extraordinary effects upon it. Whilst he was quite absorbed in his playing, a small crowd had gathered round, unperceived by him, and every one was listening with curiosity to this eccentric performance. Perhaps some of the listeners may have recognised the features of the well-known *virtuoso*. Anyhow, Langlé seized upon the opportunity for passing round the old man's hat, and collected quite a decent number of coins, which were handed to the astonished beggar, whilst Viotti got out his purse to buy the violin for twenty francs.

"Stay a moment," said the blind man, recovering a little from his surprise. "Just now I said I would sell the violin for twenty francs, but I did not know it was so good. I ought to have at least the double for it."

Viotti had never received a more genuine compliment in his life, and he did not hesitate to give the old man two gold pieces instead of one. He then walked off with the tin-plate violin under his arm.

He had scarcely gone fifty yards before he felt some one pulling at his sleeve. It was a young workman, who, touching his hat respectfully, said, "Sir, you have paid too dear for that violin; and if you are an amateur, as it was I who made it, I can supply you with as many as you like at six francs each."

This was Eustache; he had just come in time

THE ITALIAN SCHOOL 25

to hear the conclusion of the bargain, and little dreaming that he was so clever a violin-maker, no doubt desired to push forward a business so well begun.

But Viotti was quite satisfied with one sample of this merchandise. The illustrious violinist never parted with that instrument. He had it with him when he came to reside in London. It was sold at London with the other effects of the great musician after his death, and realised a few shillings only. An amateur of curiosities offered a large price to the purchaser if he, or any one else, could inform him how such a mysterious piece of workmanship came into the possession of the celebrated Viotti.

In my "Biographical Sketches of Celebrated Violinists" I said it was not known how Viotti came to be a violinist, and I could only trace his musical career from the time when, at the age of thirteen, he was placed under the celebrated Pugnani at Turin. Some have asserted, however, that he took his first lessons on the violin from his father, who was a blacksmith—truly he must have been the real "harmonious blacksmith"—and from a wandering minstrel named Giovanni, who happened to "wend his weary way" to the little Piedmontese village of Fontaneto.

This would tend to show that, like the father of Nicolo Paganini, the parent of Viotti was a musician, and had perceived a latent talent in his child that might lead to better things than are usually in store for a blacksmith. But there are blacksmiths and blacksmiths, harmonious or otherwise, some of whom have left names behind them; and it is a calling by no means to be despised. Probably this particular blacksmith was held in estimation by the aristocracy of his neighbourhood, and no doubt he shod the horses of the good Prince Pozzo; for it was this gentleman who placed the young Viotti under the care of the talented Pugnani for instruction at Turin, where he remained for many years.

'Gaetano Pugnani was one of the most brilliant stars that arose from the great Piedmontese Violin School founded by Somis, a pupil of Corelli, and chapel-master to the King of Sardinia. He was born at Turin in the year 1728, and under the excellent tuition of Somis he became a very accomplished violinist and composer, exerting no inconsiderable influence on the art of music in Northern Italy by the grandeur of his style of playing, and the improvements he introduced into the form of the Concerto.

He had already achieved much success as a soloplayer at the Court of Sardinia, before he went forth on his travels. When he arrived at Paris he had to compete with some of the greatest violinists of the period, among whom was the German *virtuoso* J. Stamitz, and the noted French artistes

THE ITALIAN SCHOOL 27

Pagin and Gaviniès. Nevertheless, Pugnani met with a very cordial reception at the *Concerts Spirituels*, where he appeared several times; and he afterwards visited many European cities, with similar successful results. He stayed for a considerable time in London, where he composed a good deal of violin music. In 1770 he was in Italy again, when Dr. Burney, the author of a "History of Music," met him at Turin, and in that city he continued the management of the Violin Academy founded by Somis.

Then it was that the boy Viotti was placed under his charge. Among his other pupils we should mention Bruni, Oliveri, Diana, Borra, Molino, Traversa, Borghi, and some others; all distinguished men in their day, whose lives, had they been handed down to us in detail, would be found surrounded, in most cases, by the halo of romance which is characteristic of artistic life, and which even the direst misery is unable to eclipse.

In his younger days Pugnani, already an accomplished violinist, experienced a great desire to see and hear Tartini, and he left Paris and proceeded to Padua for that purpose.

Tartini received him kindly, and evinced no little curiosity to hear him play. Pugnani took up a violin and commenced a "well-known" solo, but he had not played many bars before Tartini suddenly seized his arm, and said, "Too loud, my friend, too loud!"

The Piedmontese youth began again, but at the same passage Tartini stopped him again, exclaiming this time, "Too soft, my good friend, too soft!" Pugnani thereupon laid down the instrument, and begged Tartini to give him some lessons. He was at once received among the pupils of the *maestro* of Padua, and, excellent artiste as he already was, actually began his musical education over again.

I have related this anecdote in my volume above mentioned, and though there can be little doubt of its absolute correctness, I cannot help regretting not having been able, when it appeared, to name the particular "well-known" solo taken up on this occasion. It may be asserted, I think, most positively, that it was none other than the celebrated sonata, now called *Il Trillo del Diavolo*, of Tartini himself, which, as we have already seen, he had composed at the age of twenty-two, after suffering from an attack of nightmare, in which he saw and heard the eccentric performer Veracini, of Venice, in the shape of Satan, with a violin in his hand, producing the most extraordinary music. The expressive modulations in that composition are very varied from the outset, and require much care to bring out their full effect. At the time of this meeting Pugnani could have been scarcely

THE ITALIAN SCHOOL 29

more than twenty-one, and Tartini about fifty-seven years of age.

Another reason why I am certain that was the solo attempted on this occasion is that Tartini would never have taken the liberty to correct a fellow-artiste, however young, except in the performance of a piece of his own composition; he simply wished to show Pugnani how he, the composer, intended the passage to be played. If I may be allowed to go a step further, I may safely affirm that it was at the bar number six (the sixth bar from the commencement) of the sonata, which requires to be rendered somewhat softly to prepare the crescendo which follows, that the young violinist was stopped by his illustrious contemporary.

Many anecdotes have been foisted upon Pugnani, some of which bear evidence of being the creation of rivals, and are not worth repeating. Others, on the contrary, tend to enlighten us upon the character of the man. It has been stated that, when playing, he was so completely absorbed in the music that he has been known at a public concert to walk about the platform during the performance of a favourite cadenza, as if he had been at home in his own room.

His compositions are numerous, and for the most part excellent; though now they are very scarce and difficult to procure. He wrote no less than nine violin concertos, trios, quartets, quintets, and overtures. Besides all this, he was the composer of several operas which were performed with success in many of the Italian theatres. As a violinist, his style is mentioned by contemporaries as being broad and noble, endowed with all the highest qualities.

It has also been remarked that all his pupils proved to be excellent leaders. To lead well was quite a gift with Pugnani, and he possessed the art of transmitting this important accomplishment to others. With a single stroke of his bow he could correct an erroneous interpretation, or animate the lethargic performer. He even indicated to the singers on the stage the true tone and expression with which they ought to deliver their parts. As to his compositions, they are replete with melody and brilliancy.

The Parisians were jealous of Pugnani, and accused him of being a very conceited man, though the anecdote of his meeting with Tartini would go far to annihilate such an opinion. If he had been a Frenchman, he would have been lauded to the skies, or perhaps he would have had a monument at the Louvre—but an Italian ! Well, they have honoured Napoleon Buonaparte, and he was a Corsican—not to say an Italian.

The fact is that poor Pugnani was very much annoyed during his stay in the French capital. He received certain unpleasant and ill-sounding nick-

THE ITALIAN SCHOOL 31

names; and a young painter, who lived on the same flat, went so far as to take advantage of the somewhat large nose of the celebrated Piedmontese *virtuoso*, and represented him in a drawing, leading his orchestra, all the members of which were grouped under his vast nasal organ, as under an enormous parasol. Of the private life of Pugnani very little has come down to us; his name lives in his compositions and in the talents of the pupils that he instructed. Viotti owed almost everything to him, and Bruni has distinguished himself by his original and brilliant trios.

He died in Turin, the city of his birth, but the exact date is not very certain; some say 1798 and others 1803. In either case he would have been just over seventy years of age, and up to that time he was constantly engaged in composition, conducting, and teaching. Like many equally good men he "died in harness," and has left a very distinguished name in the world of Italian music.

II

THE LEADER OF THE ROYAL VIOLINS

IN the summer of 1646, when the Duc de Guise was returning from Florence to Paris, he brought back with him an Italian boy, just thirteen years of age, called Battista, but who in after life became better known as Giovanni Battista Lulli, the friend (for a time) of Molière and Louis XIV., and the founder of French opera. The lad's merry dark eyes, long flowing hair, and open countenance, together with his peculiar soft Italian accent, and, above all, his tasteful playing upon the violin, even at that early age, attracted the attention of many persons. It is said that he was engaged as a page to Mdlle. de Montpensier (niece of Louis XIV.), but that lady getting tired of him, he was given a subordinate place in the kitchen, where he soon proved a very clever cook for certain dishes then in vogue.

After some two and a half years of drudgery in the royal kitchens, enlivened occasionally by a little music, by the performance of some sprightly Italian melody, or by some wild pranks played upon the pompous *chef de cuisine*, who little dreamed that

LEADER OF THE ROYAL VIOLINS 33

one of his boys was destined to become a celebrated *chef d'orchestre*, it was discovered that "Battista" possessed an extraordinary talent for the violin. This first attracted the attention of several of the palace officials, the Comte de Nogent among others; and it led to Lulli being placed under proper tuition, and finally made a court musician.

At the age of nineteen he played for the first time before the King, and so delighted him that he was soon engaged to form a band of musicians, which was called *Les Petits Violons du Roi* (mostly formed of young men), to distinguish them from the twenty-four violinists who for some time previously had formed the band known as *Les Violons de la Chambre*. The latter had attracted the notice of our king, Charles II., and he determined to establish at the English court a similar band of violinists.

Now, at this extremely interesting and exciting period of our history, there were not many great violinists in England. It would have been exceedingly difficult, or quite impossible, in the days of Charles II., to have got together in London anything like the orchestra at Covent Garden Theatre, for instance. Nevertheless, there were two Englishmen, father and son, named Bannister, who had made for themselves in these early days considerable reputations as violin players.

John Bannister, the father, was an excellent musician, and taught his son, John the younger,

C

having been taught himself by *his* father, who used at Christmas time to play as one of the waits in the parish of St. Giles—quite a rural spot of London at that time. So, we see there was music running in the family. Well, the merry King Charles II. having formed his violin orchestra somehow or other, and got a German named Baltzar, from Lubeck, to lead it, came to hear of the talent which John Bannister displayed as a violinist, and had him forthwith sent to France to improve his musical education. On his return to England the King appointed him leader of the Royal Violins.

In Great Britain, at the time when King Charles determined upon forming a band of violinists to play to him after dinner, as he had seen done at the court of Louis XIV. during his years of exile in France, the finest performer on the violin was an amateur named David Mell, a clock-maker. Perhaps he was a very good player, but lacked that thorough knowledge of music which can only be got by a long course of study, and pertains in consequence only to those who make music their sole profession. We could certainly quote the names of many distinguished men, such as Thalberg, Bataille, Hans von Bulow, and others, who have drifted from the ranks of the amateur to those of the professional; but David Mell, fine as his performance may have been, was not offered the appointment, and the German Baltzar was sent for to lead

LEADER OF THE ROYAL VIOLINS 35

the first violin band established by an English sovereign.

An amusing old writer tells us that "after Baltzar came to England and showed his wonderful parts on that instrument, Mell was not so much admired ; yet he played sweeter, was a well-bred gentleman, and not given to excessive drinking as Baltzar was." Probably the King looked over the German musician's shortcomings in this respect; for when Baltzar died, in 1663, he was buried in Westminster Abbey, and John Bannister the elder succeeded him as leader of the Royal Violins.

It was a splendid appointment, and Bannister appears to have done ample justice to it. His contemporaries (though contemporaries are not always to be relied upon for truthful history, as many of our young literary men find out to their cost) published the opinion that this clever Englishman quite equalled the best of Italian violinists ; and one day Bannister himself actually ventured to tell King Charles that *the English violinists of his court were superior to those of the French court*, for which bold and truthful speech he lost his appointment !

This unkind action of the sovereign was not a bad thing for musicians: as soon as Bannister got his discharge he set about giving concerts, and he was *the first who established in London concerts in which the audience paid for their seats.*

Of one of these entertainments, given in 1677, we

have the announcement in which it is stated, in the language of the period, that the performance will "begin with a parley of instruments composed by Mr. Bannister, and performed by eminent masters."

John Bannister the elder died in 1679, whilst the country was reeking with popish plots, conspiracies against the King, violent political excitement, and disturbances. He also was interred in Westminster Abbey, where there was plenty of room in those days. His son, John the younger, had grown up a clever violinist like his father, and was ultimately appointed to the band of King William III.; he was also first violin at Drury Lane Theatre for many years.

With the solitary exception of David Mell, before mentioned, John Bannister the elder, leader of the Royal Violins, was the first Englishman who ever distinguished himself as a performer on the violin. He is also remarked, historically, as having been the first musician who attempted something like what we now know as a public concert. This attempt was made in the year 1672.

Roger North, who was Attorney-General under James II., left a MS. work entitled "Memoirs of Musick," which was published after his death. In this work we are told that "John Bannister had a good theatrical vein, and in composition he had a lively style peculiar to himself. He possessed a large room at Whyte Friars, next to Temple Bar Gate, and made a large raised box for the musicians, whose modesty required curtains. This room was rounded with small tables—alehouse fashion. One shilling was the price, and call for what you pleased; there was very good music, for Bannister found means to procure the best hands in towne, and some voices to come and perform there; and there wanted no variety of humour, for Bannister himself (*inter alia*) did wonders upon the flageolet to thoro' bass, and the several masters had their solos. This continued full one winter, and more I remember not."

We know, however, that these concerts continued for many years. The first of all, which took place on the 30th September 1672, was announced as follows :—"These are to give notice that at Mr. John Bannister's house (now called the *Music School*) over against *The George Tavern* in Whyte Friars, this present Monday will be performed musick by excellent masters, beginning precisely at four o'clock in the afternoon, and every afternoon for the future precisely at the same hour." That announcement appeared in the *London Gazette*, 30th September 1672. A younger contemporary of Bannister, a musician named Shuttleworth, whose father was a teacher of music in Spitalfields, afterwards led similar concerts at *The Swan Tavern* in Cornhill, in 1735; and in process of time others followed, until concerts became general throughout Great Britain, thanks to the happy initiative of John Bannister, the leader of the Royal Violins.

III

CHERUBINI AS A VIOLINIST

MANY of my readers will be surprised to find the celebrated composer Luigi Cherubini mentioned as a violinist. However, a man may be a tolerably good performer on the violin without attaining to anything approaching celebrity in that capacity. But the author of *Lodoiska, Medea, The Water Carriers, Anacreon,* and a host of other operatic and religious works, did really know something of the secrets of the violin, and, in fact, it may be safely asserted that he owed his life to that very circumstance.

Among other well-known composers of opera, I may mention that Balfe began his career as a violinist, and so did Auber ; and this may go far to explain the melodious scores of the composers of *The Bohemian Girl* and *Fra Diavolo.*

Maybe it was Cherubini's love for this wonderful instrument that helped to make him so intimate with the great *virtuoso* Viotti, with whom he resided at Paris for three whole years—not, indeed, for the sake of violin lessons. This intimacy was chiefly

CHERUBINI AS A VIOLINIST

due to the fact that they were both Italians, living in a foreign land, where they were duly recognised as two of the finest musicians of that day.

At Florence, where Cherubini was born in 1760, and where he received his first lessons in solfeggio and the harpsichord from his worthy father, Bartolomeo Cherubini, *maestro al clavicembalo* at the Pergola Theatre, the hard-working parent of twelve children, of whom Luigi was the tenth, the family resided in a modest cottage in the Via Fiesolana. When about eight or nine years of age, this tenth child Luigi found in the house what one of his biographers terms a "wretched" old violin, and "amused himself by scraping on it."

Please, dear reader, take note of the date—say 1768 or 1769—and the country—Tuscany, not very far from the celebrated violin-making city of Cremona!

A "wretched violin"! Who can say, if the said instrument were now in the hands of a London dealer, it would not be considered cheap at £500 or £600?

In Northern Italy, at that time, it is doubtful whether such a thing as a "wretched old violin" could have existed.

Only just fancy the thousands of pounds sterling that have been spent in buying up the Italian violins of that period!

It was probably an Amati, or a Stradivari, with a

pure, soft, yet brilliant tone; and the boy's naturally musical ears were, doubtless, pleased by the sound, even such as it was yielded by his own rough and inexperienced handling of the instrument. It is certain that he must have persevered, though who taught him we know not, unless it were his clever father.

But the fact is preserved that, although the violin is justly considered to be a most difficult instrument to learn, young Cherubini in less than two years was able, one evening, when a violinist was absent from the orchestra, to accompany his father to the theatre, and take the place of the missing man. It is even recorded that he played his part throughout so well that Nardini, the conductor, could find no fault save "a certain timidity and hesitation," only natural under the circumstances of a first appearance in public.

We hear no more of Cherubini as a performer on the violin until many years later, after he had quitted his native Italy and paid one or two visits to London as a composer on the highway to fame, and had finally fixed his residence at Paris. It was at the time of the great French Revolution; and the fact of his having learnt to play the violin when a child was the means of saving his life in the hour of danger.

His compositions, though far too learned for the light French taste, had by the year 1790, when he

CHERUBINI AS A VIOLINIST 41

began to write an opera for Louis XVI., on the subject of *Marguerite d'Anjou*, firmly established his reputation as one of the greatest musicians of the period.

But when the Revolution broke out, Cherubini's prospects became almost as clouded as those of the Monarchy. His position depended to a great extent upon the aristocracy, who patronised him as he deserved; but now these noble friends were flying from France, or being murdered by the mob.

During the first four years of anarchy he suffered great distress. Forced to live in seclusion, his livelihood became precarious, and his time was passed chiefly in the study of music and botany (a branch of science of which he was extremely fond) without remuneration, and anxiously awaiting the advent of better days.

He was compelled to limit his acquaintance, in those horrible times, to a very few trustworthy friends, musicians like himself, on whom he could thoroughly rely, and among whom there was not one who, by denouncing him as an aristocrat or a royalist, would have caused him, like so many equally good men, to be slaughtered on the scaffold at a few hours' notice.

Even to stir out of doors was a risky thing to do, for reckless mobs of half-drunken anarchists rolled along the streets day and night, seeking to satisfy their rapacious longings for the blood of respected citizens and for their goods.

Once, during an occasion of more than ordinary excitement, Cherubini fell into the hands of a band of these raving robbers, who were seeking for musicians to conduct their revolutionary howlings. To them it was a special satisfaction to compel men of talent, who had formerly delighted royalty and nobility, to administer now to their own gratification. On the great composer firmly refusing to lead them, a murmur ran through the crowd, and he was taunted by half a dozen voices as being a "royalist." Such a taunt had only to be taken up by the remainder, to signify speedy death.

At this intensely critical moment, one of Cherubini's friends, a musician who had already been forcibly enrolled by the ruffians, and happened to be standing near him, thrust a "wretched violin" into his unwilling hands, and by most earnest entreaties finally induced him to lead the anarchist mob.

The whole of the day these two unfortunate musicians were compelled to accompany the howling fanatics; and when at last a halt was made in one of the squares, where a "banquet" was given, Cherubini and his friend were made to stand on two empty barrels and play away till the feast, or farce, was finished. It is impossible to realise

CHERUBINI AS A VIOLINIST 43

anything more horribly ludicrous! That was Cherubini's last performance on the violin.

In 1792 the talented Viotti fled to England; and in 1793, just over a hundred years ago, when the storm had burst in all its fury, and the unfortunate, good-natured king, at the age of thirty-eight, mounted the scaffold, Cherubini had taken refuge at the country house of a friend, an architect, near Rouen, where he lived in tranquillity and safety, and only returned to Paris the following year.

In 1795 he was made inspector of the newly formed Conservatoire, a musical school which was an offshoot of the Revolution, and from that time forward his position was assured. His great talent and perseverance enabled him to conquer all obstacles, even the hatred and jealousy of the *Petit Caporal* himself.

Why Napoleon Buonaparte should have detested Cherubini, and persecuted him in the way he did, it is not easy to imagine. But nothing less than the greatest talent could have resisted such noxious influence.

Those who wish to see how the middle classes, bankers, lawyers, musicians, &c., fared during the great French Revolution, I may refer to my "Scenes from the Reign of Louis XVI." (London : Bentley & Son, 1878).

IV

THE SECRET OF PAGANINI

THAT Paganini had a greater share of success than any violinist who preceded him will be readily admitted, just as we may say that Shakespeare as a writer of plays stood far above any of his predecessors. Paganini had a natural gift for music nearly as great as that of our "immortal Will" for blank verse. He inherited it from his father, and, probably, also from his mother, who were both known in Genoa to be great votaries of the divine art. After this gift had been duly cultivated, it enabled him to astonish his contemporaries by his performances on the violin and on the guitar.

When we remember that his father was a clever player on the mandoline, the latter accomplishment is less surprising; but the details of the boyish life of Nicolo Paganini are little known, except that he appears to have been *severely* encouraged in his music by the said father, and kindly treated by his mother. He was of a highly nervous and sensitive nature, and was taught, while still very young, by his stern parent, who was but a poor clerk in a

THE SECRET OF PAGANINI 45

shipping office, that it is necessary to persevere and to push oneself forward to secure success, or even a decent living. There was a certain amount of cunning also in his character; and that he took advantage of every opportunity that offered was manifest already in his youth, when he was easily induced, not only to forsake the modest paternal roof, but to try his hand at the gaming-table as well as in the concert room.

Add to these attributes of Paganini the fact that he was well instructed when quite a young boy in the rudiments of music, compelled by his relentless father to work hard at his exercises—too hard, indeed, for it injured his health and moral character—and, later, that he had some of the best lessons in harmony and composition that Italy could afford in his day, and we find much to account for his wonderfully successful career and the £80,000 that he left to his only son.

But beyond all this, we have been assured by more than one writer that Paganini carried with him to the grave *an important secret* which alone would explain, if not the whole of his success, at least nine-tenths of it.

The late Professor Fétis, of the Brussels Conservatoire, who had some knowledge of the violin, and was a most ardent admirer of Paganini, whom he did not quite understand, believed that no such secret could possibly exist. We shall see! He asserted, doubtless with much truth, that there is no royal road to brilliant execution, and that nothing but downright hard work, combined with an extraordinary natural gift, could account for the wonderful impression Paganini made in the world of music, and on violinists in particular.

On the other hand, we are reminded that the violoncellist Ciandelli, who was very kind to Paganini during one of his attacks of illness at Naples, and who was known to be a very indifferent soloist, though a good musician and orchestral player, had given to him by the great Genoese artiste, in return for this kindness, some insight into the secret in question, and was thereby transformed, in less than a fortnight, from a very mediocre performer into a *virtuoso* of the first rank.

Let us add to this, that among the very few persons to whom Nicolo Paganini gave any instruction, the young girl, Signora Calcagno, of Genoa, astonished the musical world in that part of Europe by the boldness and brilliancy of her playing; and some time afterwards, the late Camillo Sivori, one of the finest, if not the very finest violin player ever heard, and of whom I shall speak again in this volume, also made a great and lasting impression.

That this secret existed more in the actual execution than in the composition of the works performed may be taken for granted; for, on scrutinising the compositions of Paganini, it is clear that

THE SECRET OF PAGANINI 47

he had not a great gift of melody, such as we find so conspicuous in the popular composers of Italy. Most of his themes are borrowed, and upon these he scored wonderfully effective variations—a style now almost gone out of fashion. When he is entirely original in this respect, he is often very mediocre ; but he is always dramatic.

In order to exhibit in as clear a light as possible the nature of this secret—for secret there certainly was, as all my readers will eventually discover—it is necessary to look a little into the life and surroundings of the great Genoese violinist. It will be found that the laborious and highly meritorious work of Guhr, of Frankfort, who attempted to explain him, is to a great extent beside the mark ; and that the absurd scoring of the *double harmonics* by the editors of the cheap editions of Paganini's works is merely theoretical, quite impossible in practice, and not at all as Paganini played them.

It has more than once been asserted that our "wily Italian," as he was sometimes called, took his new ideas from the writings of a pupil of Corelli, named Locatelli, who more than any others went beyond the teaching of his master. But let any of my readers take some of these compositions and compare them with those of Paganini, and they will soon perceive that, though the latter may possibly have seen them, he has certainly not imitated them at all. In Paganini's music the phrasing is most natural, and eminently suited to the instrument, whilst Locatelli seems to have laboured to place the fingers of the left hand in the most difficult positions that his limited acquaintance with the resources of the violin could possibly conceive, and to have cultivated as much as he could what has been humorously termed "the art of playing out of tune."

Fancy a composer inserting at the head of a piece of music the words, " Easy to read, difficult to execute," as we read on one of Locatelli's pieces ! What is the use of making music unnecessarily difficult ? The nightingale, the lark, and the thrush are conscious of no difficulty; nor will the *virtuoso* who experiences difficulty in his performance ever entrance his public. What most astonished the audience of Paganini was the consummate ease with which the most daring passages were executed.

It is customary to look upon Paganini as the creator of the modern school of violin playing. This is not at all a just notion. In the first place, we must remember the distinguished men who immediately preceded him, among whom the more conspicuous were Viotti, Rode, Giornowick, Kreutzer, &c.; and especially must we note the contemporaries of the Genoese artiste, men who were, like himself, all competing at the same time on the concert platform for public favour, and among

THE SECRET OF PAGANINI 49

whom the greatest were De Bériot, Spohr, Lafont, and Lipinski.

If we glance at the careers of these men, and the compositions which they have left us, it is very easy to see that Paganini was not quite so much of a pioneer as many persons appear to believe. That he had certain well-marked characteristics, and that his performance was in the highest degree dramatic, cannot be denied; and whether we look at his compositions, or consider the style in which they were performed, it is impossible not to award him the very first place among the violinists of his period. All other performers, even the great Spohr and the charming Lafont, were utterly tame in comparison with him.

Louis Spohr was born the same year as Paganini, 1784; but De Bériot was much younger, having been born in 1802; and it was very fortunate for the latter that he made his appearance in London *a few years previous to the arrival of Paganini*.

The three pieces of music which contain *the whole secret* of Paganini's style and manner of performance may be briefly enumerated as *Le Stregghe*, the *Rondo de la Clochette*, and the *Carnaval de Venise*. They were evidently, for many years, his favourite solos; and nearly all his other works may be looked upon as more or less inferior imitations, or reproductions of them. All that he knew of the violin, everything that he did, is contained in these three

D

works, which have, fortunately, come down to us completely intact, just as he left them in MS. They were sold to the well-known publishers, Schott Brothers, by the son of Paganini, and have been printed with extreme care.

Many spurious compositions, including the *Merveille de Paganini*, which appeared in Guhr's book, have been published from time to time; but Paganini denied the authorship of them in his lifetime. We wonder what he would have said had he been able to see the notation of the double-harmonic passages to the *Non piu mesta*, or *Le Stregghe* and other works, as given in some of the German editions of his music! They would certainly have raised a smile on his pale, melancholy countenance, more sarcastical than any which he usually bestowed on his audience.

All this nonsensical scoring is, of course, absent from the real edition of Paganini's works published by Schott Brothers.

The mother of Nicolo Paganini once had a dream which she related to her young son in these terms: —"My child, you will be a great musician. An angel radiant with beauty appeared to me during the night, and promised to accomplish any wish I might make. *I requested that you should be the greatest of all violinists*, and the angel granted that my desire should be fulfilled."

Whether this little speech was imagined for the

sake of encouraging her son to work, and to enable him to endure the harsh treatment of his father, or whether it was a real dream—which is more probable—a sort of instinctive foreshadowing in the mother's mind of her child's future career, always present in her thoughts, might prove a subject of discussion; but it is certain that the angel "radiant with beauty" did keep the promise in the most perfect manner, for Nicolo Paganini was, without doubt, the most wonderful violinist of the first half of this century.

Antonio Paganini, his father, was, as we intimated above, a ship-broker's clerk, who was passionately fond of music and played on the mandoline. We know little about him, except that he soon perceived his child's gift, and made the naturally delicate young creature study prematurely, and so hard that he turned him out a very tolerable soloist at six years of age!

The boy certainly gave evidence of very precocious skill, and was, even at this early period of his life, fond of striving after peculiar effects, calculated to astonish his hearers.

But his father's knowledge of music was rather limited, and he could do no more than inculcate the rudest elements of the art. He therefore induced the leader of the orchestra at the Genoa theatre, a violinist named Cervetto, to give the child some instruction during his leisure moments; and two years later, when eight years of age, the young Paganini was placed under Giacomo Costa, who was director of Church music at Genoa, and a very able violinist. Costa gave him lessons for about six months, and made him play occasionally in the orchestra during divine service. At the same time the composer Gnecco befriended the poor lad, and gave him some hints on harmony.

It has been stated that the ambitious young Nicolo actually composed his first piece—a kind of sonata, now lost like many other of his compositions—when he was not quite nine years of age. And from the very first he began by playing his own music, a habit that he adhered to throughout his entire career.

Thus, in the first concert in which he ever appeared, when about nine years old, he performed some variations which he himself had composed on a French air of the period. This concert was given in the theatre at Genoa by two well-known singers, who afterwards sang for his benefit in a second concert.

So we see that instinct led the Genoese artiste from the very outset of his career to perform his own music. If he took up any other compositions, as he once remarked in after-life, he had to arrange them to suit his own style of performance, and this was quite as much trouble to him as writing a new piece. Once, in order to please the Parisians, he

THE SECRET OF PAGANINI 53

attempted to play the *Seventh Concerto* of Pierre Rode, and, we are assured, the performance was beneath mediocrity!

All these little details must be taken into account to enable me to elucidate the object I have in view, namely, to exhibit the cause of Paganini's wonderfully successful career; in other words, to make known his secret.

Generally speaking, when a student of music proceeds from one professor to another, if the latter is really the more eminent in his profession, all the teaching of the former is laid aside or forgotten, but not entirely lost. It was no doubt the twanging of his father's mandoline which originated Paganini's love of pizzicato passages, and led to his proficiency as a guitar player, for which instrument he forsook the violin for about three years.

When twelve years of age his father took him to Alessandro Rolla, who was a well-known professor of the violin at Parma; and although the latter said that the boy already knew all he could teach him, it was agreed that he should remain with him as a pupil for a twelvemonth, during which time he studied the art of composition under Ghiretti and his pupil Paër (afterwards a celebrated composer of operas), who was very kind to him; and in 1797, when thirteen years old, Nicolo Paganini returned to Genoa.

There we have all that is known regarding the

teaching of the boy Paganini. Instruction ceased when he was only thirteen; all the rest is due to his own initiative, to his natural gift for music, and his indomitable determination to shine as a brilliant *virtuoso*. Nevertheless, short as his career of instruction was, it laid down a good, healthy foundation; we can feel the influence of these invaluable lessons of Ghiretti and Paër on almost every page of music that Paganini wrote.

There have been so many errors, and downright falsehoods, published about Paganini, many of which he quietly allowed to circulate without any contradiction—because the "wily Italian" knew perfectly well that they would only serve to advertise his name, and to draw crowds of people to his concerts—that it is no easy task to get at the real man as nature made him and art perfected him.

The great difficulty of Paganini's music is generally uppermost in men's minds when this genius of the violin happens to come forward in conversation; but though it was, doubtless, extremely difficult, and quite incomprehensible for the period in which he lived, when most violinists, like the immortal Corelli, rarely ventured beyond the third position, it loses much of this quality when compared with the music performed by many modern violinists. I could point to pieces by Prume, Wieniawski, and my old friend, the late Henri

Vieuxtemps, among others, that are quite as difficult as anything that Paganini wrote. All these were men who delighted more to astonish than to charm. Indeed, there are many *virtuosi* who find it difficult or impossible to charm, and for them such music is most appropriate.

As the art of violin playing, like all other branches of art, progresses year by year, so at the present day we find a notable number of artistes that have ventured to play the compositions of Paganini in their concerts, who, had they lived fifty or sixty years ago, could not have attempted such a thing. This may be taken as a word of compliment to our modern professors, some of whom are really giants in the land.

Nevertheless, I have known a simple but charming melody played by a pretty girl of eighteen summers, who really could make her violin vibrate in accordance with the poetry in her heart, bring forth bursts of applause as loud and prolonged as were ever awarded to the most intricate compositions of the greatest masters. Music, as the voice of love and nature, knows no difficulties, as I have before hinted; but a little of the demon in it, now and then, does no harm.

Now Paganini, from the very beginning, was all demon, not only in his dramatic playing, but in his unusually weird appearance. If he ever failed, it was precisely in those cantabile passages which are necessary to connect together the outbursts of rapid and passionate execution. Thus he sometimes displeased the Neapolitans and Venetians, who from birth are inured to their lovely popular melodies and the luscious songs of the gondoliers.

We have seen that by thirteen years of age all tuition, as far as masters are concerned, had ceased for him; and everything beyond this early instruction is due to his own personal efforts.

It is a lesson to those who imagine that a master can do everything, and who constantly fly from one teacher to another in the hope of being made perfect by others instead of perfecting themselves. *Aide toi, et Dieu t'aidera*, should be the motto of all young violinists. Masters are indispensable, but most depends upon the student's own efforts, and all does not consist in conquering mechanical difficulties.

Let us see what Paganini did in the way of improving himself between the years of thirteen and twenty-four, when he published his curious *Ventri quattri Caprici* (Twenty-four Caprices), which had no more success with the violinists of that day than the outrageous fantasias imagined by Locatelli, of which mention has already been made.

When he returned to Genoa in 1797, he began at this early age to write his first compositions for the violin, and to practise assiduously every day. As time went on he wrote his music so difficult that

THE SECRET OF PAGANINI 57

it required all his energy to master it, and he was occasionally seen or heard to try the same passage in a hundred different ways, until he had discovered the best means of performing it; so that at the end of the day he used to fall in a state of complete exhaustion upon a couch, where he would lie quite motionless for a considerable time.

His ambitious father now determined upon taking him on a professional tour through the principal towns of Lombardy.

The science of the music agent was not so developed in those days as it is now, and a private individual could "go on tour," on his own account, without all those risks and troubles that have cropped up as competition and an ever-increasing number of "wandering minstrels" have made their appearance. A man of some talent could make a comfortable income, if not a large fortune, in the principal towns of his own country. Now the greatest of artistes must wander over the whole world.

Though Paganini was yet a child, this tour in Lombardy was successful enough to impress him with the idea that he might just as well make such a journey by himself alone, and so shake off the disagreeable trammels of an exacting parent. He had been flattered and pampered by all who came in contact with him, and applauded to the skies; so the precocious lad, who was not a bad-looking young fellow, took the very first opportunity of freeing himself from the restraint of a father whom he dreaded rather than loved.

As a great deal of his music has been lost, it is impossible to say what he played on these occasions. We are certain of one thing only, that it was his own composition; and we shall see how much this enhanced his reputation and fostered success.

There is no harm, as many pedants have pretended, in an artiste playing his own music, provided it is good, and gives people satisfaction. The illustrious Rossini long ago said that he only recognised *two kinds of music*—that which is good, and that which is bad. In Paganini's case it was *better* than any violin music then generally heard, and gave more than satisfaction, for people went into delirium about it—or about him.

He in great measure created the difficulties which he performed, and later in life he rarely or ever studied. Having done so much when young, he could then afford to repose. But having once accustomed himself to the most brilliant and difficult of music, it was to him, ever afterwards, very little more than child's play.

The most florid and effective passages in his music are so natural, so perfectly suited to the instrument, that it is easy to imagine little labour would have been required in after-life to keep them up. In this respect he differed from most violinists, ancient or modern. He was the first to develop the full resources of the violin as a solo instrument, and his successors have largely profited by his labours.

As a solo player Paganini was the greatest violinist the world has known, or probably ever will know; because, joined to his wonderful facility of execution and perfect knowledge of harmony, he possessed a natural gift for music and a peculiar nervous organisation which enabled him to carry it out to the fullest extent. His long fingers were advantageous for extended passages, and enabled him to take tenths and other intervals with greater ease than violinists in general can command. They also enabled him to rise with facility in his double-stopping to the highest notes of the instrument. His ear was most sensitive, and hence his intonation was marvellously just. Sometimes his nervous frenzy got the better of him, and his harmonic passages are said to have grated on the nerves of the ladies at the court of the Princess Bacciochi, at Lucca, where he frequently played during his appointment there as organiser of concerts and leader of the orchestra.

He wrote all his pieces in the easiest keys of the violin; but as he often mounted his A by half a tone, to make his violin more brilliant, the accompaniment was, of course, in a different key.

He used very thin strings, not only because he

found they suited his Guarnerius violin and gave a finer tone, but also because they rendered the pizzicato passages easier to perform.

He was very clever and effective with his pizzicato, and sometimes performed it with both hands, as in one of the variations of his *Carnaval*, which is entirely executed in this manner. His double harmonics, which have intrigued all modern violinists without exception, were played on the bridge, *sul ponticello;* he indicates them in the score by the word "armonioso," and he has unintentionally let out the secret in his wonderful piece, *Le Stregghe* (The Witches), but nobody seems hitherto to have discovered it. He had acquired a wonderful dexterity in this respect; and these harmonic tones can be played even a little distance from the bridge. By long practice *a stroke of the bow* can be acquired that will produce the harmonics of the notes stopped by the fingers. It is not, in this case, the finger, but the bow that rests lightly on the strings, to produce this harmonic effect. It is often more surprising than agreeable. In this way he played the passages in double harmonics in all his pieces where they are indicated, and the curious *echo* effects in the *Rondo de la Clochette* and the *Carnaval de Venise*. De Bériot imitated this peculiar effect to a certain extent in the second variation of his beautiful *Ninth Air Varié*, but he separated the two notes instead of striking them both together.

THE SECRET OF PAGANINI 61

When Paganini used staccato passages, which was not often, it was invariably with the jumping bow, not the stiff classic staccato which forms such a beautiful ornament in modern violin playing. This, as with some other eminent violinists we could mention, he had never acquired. In performing a staccato scale with the elastic or jumping bow, he occasionally failed, according to the evidence of his contemporaries, in making the stroke of the bow and fall of the fingers coincide exactly.

He had devoted much attention to the fourth string—urged to do so in the first instance at the court at Lucca—and played whole pieces on this one string alone, making use of the natural and artificial harmonics to lengthen the scale. This was an entire novelty. In this respect he has been much imitated by modern players. In De Bériot's *Second Air Varié*, one of the most beautiful and effective that he ever wrote, the theme and one variation are entirely written for the fourth string, which is raised half a tone for the occasion, just in the style of Paganini.

The Genoese artiste's knowledge of the violin was not superior to that of his younger contemporary just named. On the contrary, the double-stopping in many of De Bériot's Concertos and his harmonic effects are occasionally finer than anything that has issued from the pen of Paganini. Moreover, in the *Eighth Air*, and his *Second Concerto*, De Bériot makes use of a style of artificial harmonic which appears to have been quite unknown to Paganini; at least, we find it in none of his writings.

In chords and arpeggio passages, octaves and tenths, there is nothing particular to be said as regards the great Italian violinist, except that he was almost a pioneer in this kind of execution, or, at least, the first to make effective use of it in the concert room. The same remark will hold good for Paganini's music as compared with that of Ernst. The latter is very elegant and extremely brilliant; but in this respect he is but an imitator of the Italian. His *Carnaval* is very effective, more beautiful, perhaps, than that of the latter, but Paganini's affords the broadest tone and most dramatic style. That of Ernst is somewhat thin in comparison. The same may also be said of Paganini's *Sonatas*, especially No. XII. (of Alard's collection). In this, as in all his other music, a fine broad tone is bound to come out in the hands of an artiste. This is rather remarkable, because it has been said that Paganini's tone was delicate rather than fine, and that in fulness of tone he was surpassed by Baillot, De Bériot, and, perhaps, by Lafont.

Paganini played upon a Guarneri violin, which responded brilliantly to all the varied effects to which I have alluded, though, from what we have learned, it was not absolutely devoid of a slight

THE SECRET OF PAGANINI 63

nasal quality, which displeased some of his hearers when, in one of his nervous frenzies, he glided slowly from one note to another. It is said that an uncouth hissing effect was thus produced that was anything but pleasant.

The main success of his brilliant performance was due to the fact of his writing his solo music in the keys best suited to the violin, and so making the chords and passages the most natural and effective possible. Great as was his execution, he could only shine in playing his own music—this in spite of some wonderful stories that have been told as to his playing at sight, and the fact that for some few years he conducted the court orchestra at Lucca.

I think I have now shown in what consisted the secret of Paganini, so far as actual music is concerned. His peculiar appearance and cunning character had, of course, much to do with his success. For a fuller account of his wonderful career I must refer to my volume, " Biographical Sketches of Celebrated Violinists."

V

THE VIOLIN DAYS OF BALFE

"THE most popular of our English composers is an Irishman," said a gentleman, who must have had a little Irish blood in his veins also.

With regard to popularity nothing could be more true. The flowing melodies of Balfe and his effective operatic music will live for many long years yet, probably as long as those of Mozart or Rossini. He got his inspiration from the melodious Italian school. The young Bellini was his contemporary for a short time, and his model for song. Hence the reminiscences of *La Sonnambula* which occur in the *Maid of Artois* and elsewhere. He relied for his orchestration upon a good knowledge of the successful works of his day, and a natural talent for composition.

Balfe was a far more complete musician than many of our contemporaries appear to believe. He certainly had genius, and what he may have lacked in this respect he made up by perseverance and hard work, actuated no doubt by ardent ambition.

THE VIOLIN DAYS OF BALFE 65

His career is a very interesting one. We have no violinist either in England or abroad who has ever produced so popular a work as the *Bohemian Girl*, with the sole exception of Auber, the celebrated composer of *Fra Diavolo* and *Massaniello*, who, like Balfe, also began life as a violin player.

We owe the long list of operas which have issued from Balfe's lyrical pen to the circumstance that he was the son of a violinist, who soon recognised a passionate love for music in his child.

Born at Dublin in 1808, Michael William Balfe was, at a very early age, put through a course of violin instruction by his father, who brought him on as far as he was able—and at a time when his delicate health made the task of teaching extremely irksome, but it was a labour of love—and then handed the boy over to a bandmaster named Meadows. But a little later he was transferred to Rooke, the composer of a once well-known opera called *Amelie, or the Love Test*.

Like many eminent violinists whom we could mention, Balfe made his first public appearance at the age of eight, with a violin that appeared nearly as large as himself. It was in May 1816 that Rooke brought him out at a concert in Dublin, when the lad performed, with remarkable success, a composition by Mayseder.

This appearance had the effect of attracting the attention of certain fashionable patrons to the youthful violinist; but much does not seem to have come of it.

The boy soon passed out of the hands of Rooke to those of James Barton, and the better known Alexander Lee, from whom he obtained a very fair knowledge of thorough-bass. At the same time his curiosity attracted him to several other orchestral instruments, and to the piano.

At nine years of age Balfe composed a little song, which was sung by the celebrated Madame Vestris in one of her successful characters. Years afterwards, but whilst still quite young, he used to crawl into the gallery of a London theatre to hear his own song, and revel in the applause which invariably followed it. It was published under the title of *The Lover's Mistake,* and we believe that all Balfe got in the way of remuneration was a parcel of twenty copies, to give away, or sell, as he might think proper. Very different were the circumstances many years afterwards when he composed that beautiful song with French words, *Si tu savais*, generally known as "Balfe's Air," and so popular even on the Continent, that one day the composer being introduced to a Parisian lady of fashion who spoke a little English, she inquired, "*Are you Mr. Balfe of the Air?*"

For about six years the lad continued to study with assiduity, occasionally accepting an engagement to play at concerts. At Dublin he was already

THE VIOLIN DAYS OF BALFE 67

looked upon by the public as a violinist of established repute, distinguished for the correctness and intelligence of his playing, no less than for the grace and feeling he threw into the slightest passages, when his excellent father died. This was in 1823; Balfe was then only fifteen years of age.

Charles Horn (son of the composer), a well-known singer, was in Dublin at the time, and he had heard young Balfe play a violin solo. He was on the eve of his departure for London, when the boy paid him a visit, and begged to be taken there with him. Horn proposed that he should be articled to him for seven years, and the proposition was accepted.

The future composer of the *Rose of Castille*, the *Bohemian Girl*, and the *Maid of Artois* soon got a position in the orchestra of Drury Lane for the so-called Oratorio Concerts which were given during Lent. He rose rapidly to the rank of first violin in those concerts, and played solos on alternate nights with Mori, already an eminent performer. These violin solos were the most attractive items in the programme.

This was a very high position for so young a musician, and his ambition led him to work hard in order to keep it. When the Oratorio Concerts ceased, Horn procured for his young friend an engagement in the Drury Lane orchestra during the theatrical season.

The witty and jovial Tom Cooke, quite a celebrity

in his day, was then conductor of the music at Drury Lane, and he soon recognised the remarkable capacity of the youthful violinist. Many a time, during Cooke's absence from indisposition or other causes, did young Balfe wield the *bâton*, and it is said that he quite eclipsed his conductor on these occasions.

Not long afterwards Balfe began to study under C. F. Horn (the father of the singer who had brought him from Dublin), organist of the Chapel Royal at Windsor, and a clever composer. Under his able tuition he acquired in a very short time a truly marvellous talent for composition, and could complete a full and effective instrumental score to any melody with remarkable ease and rapidity. We know that the celebrated Mozart scored most of the overture to the *Flauto Magico* whilst playing a game of skittles. Balfe appears to have possessed a similar facility.

With all this, his life in London was not precisely a bed of roses. More than once he was the dupe of impostors, who made use of his early talents as a composer to serve their own ends, and he had a fair share of hardships and privations.

The members of the Drury Lane orchestra were also engaged for a series of concerts at Vauxhall Gardens, then a fashionable *suburb* of London. It was during these engagements that Balfe somehow discovered that he possessed a tolerably good bari-

THE VIOLIN DAYS OF BALFE 69

tone voice. It was a voice of considerable compass, but of only moderate power and quality. Nevertheless he determined to cultivate it, and with this object he went through a course of vocal studies.

The result of this was, that in about a year he decided upon trying his fortune as a singer and actor. He made his first attempt in this direction at a theatre in Norwich, as Caspar in Weber's opera, *Der Freyschutz*. The attempt was a failure—not due entirely, however, to his want of experience and vocal power, but partly to an alarm of fire during the incantation scene.

So Balfe returned to the orchestra at Drury Lane, though he still retained his idea of coming out as a dramatic singer. But the thought of maturing his vocal and theatrical studies under the genial Italian sky entered his mind at this period, and he began to study the French and Italian languages.

His most ardent desires were eventually realised by a very romantic freak of fortune, entirely due to his violin.

Being introduced at a little musical party to a wealthy Italian nobleman, Count Mazzara, this gentleman was not only enchanted by Balfe's violin playing, but found in the young Irishman such a striking likeness to a dearly-loved son whom he had recently lost, that he became a most kind friend and patron, taking young Balfe to Italy with him, introducing him on the way to Cherubini at Paris, and finally placing him under the tuition of Frederici at Milan.

Balfe was then only eighteen years of age. It was at Milan that he made his maiden attempt at dramatic composition, and laid the foundation of his subsequent successful career. His violin was now laid aside for the pen.

But in spite of the satisfactory success of his first piece, a ballet, he found himself compelled to again try his fortune as an operatic singer. To follow the ultimate career of the celebrated composer would occupy a large volume if we wished to trace him, step by step, through his friendship with Cherubini and Rossini, his singing at the Italian Opera in Paris, his interesting career in Italy, Germany, and England. Balfe the violinist now entirely made way for Balfe the singer.

We are informed on very good authority that Rossini was so surprised at Balfe's singing of the *Largo al factotum*, in *Il Barbiere*, that he induced Gallois, the rich banker, to support him for one year whilst he went through an artistic training under the celebrated Bordogni (author of the beautiful studies for *Contralto*, which were originally composed for Balfe), and then got him an engagement as baritone for three years at the Italian Opera in Paris, at the rate of £600 for the first year, £800 for the second, and £1000 for the third. Balfe was then little over twenty years of age.

THE VIOLIN DAYS OF BALFE 71

Henceforth his career as an operatic singer was very successful ; but his ardent ambition to succeed as a composer was as strong as ever. Henrietta Sontag and the charming and clever Madame Malibran (soon to be the wife of De Bériot) sang often in the same operas with him. Malibran was instrumental in helping him to bring out an opera in London, and his *Siege of Rochelle* (October 29th, 1835) was a phenomenal success ; it ran for seventy nights. The *Maid of Artois*, in which Malibran sang with such marvellous effect, was still more successful, bringing into the treasury £5690 in the course of the first fortnight.

The violin was by this time enclosed for ever in its case, never again to serve its former master, whom it had thus aided, like some enchanted talisman, up the ladder of fame. No, not *never!* One of his last violin exploits occurred in Italy, at Pavia, where the well-known baritone, Signor Balfe, was engaged to sing the part of Pharaoh in Rossini's *Mosè in Egitto;* but another part was unexpectedly assigned to him. The conductor's health failing at the time, Balfe was deputed to produce the opera in question. At rehearsal the violins had been upbraided on account of their careless execution of a certain passage, when the leader exclaimed, indignantly, that it was "no violin passage at all."

"Not a violin passage !" retorted Balfe. "Do you imagine that Rossini did not know what he was about ?"

To which the leading violin impertinently replied, " You come here and play it, and I will go on and sing for you."

Whereupon Balfe snatched up a violin, and played the passage so skilfully that it elicited the unanimous applause of all present.

The romantic career of Balfe, and his wonderful success in London, Paris, Milan, Vienna, Berlin, and St. Petersburg, form a most interesting study, which we recommend to all young and aspiring musicians. A tolerably good account of this, and a list of his works, will be found in Charles Lamb Kenny's " Life of Balfe." In the early part of the present century he was doubtless the most brilliant musical star that had ever arisen in the firmament of Great Britain, and his admirable character as a son, a husband, and a father, quite as much as his musical genius, well deserves the fine statue which has been placed in the entrance-hall of Drury Lane Theatre.

Scores of interesting anecdotes of Balfe are to be found in the two little volumes of " Musical Reminiscences," published many years ago by Henry Phillips, the great English baritone, also a friend of the celebrated Malibran ; and in a more recent work by W. Beale, a member of the well-known musical firm, Cramer, Beale & Co., of Regent Street, London.

VI

CHARLES AUGUSTE DE BÉRIOT

(1802-1870)

LONG before the Revolution of 1830, Brussels was the city of Flanders where the best music was to be heard, and no Continental town has had a more successful Conservatoire, more particularly as regards the violin, the violoncello, and the piano. As a school for singing it has been much less successful, though it has given our opera houses Madame Lemmens-Sherrington, Mademoiselle Artot, Mademoiselle Singelée, Madame Lauters, and a few others well worthy of note.

A new school for the violin was formed there in the early part of the present century, under the auspices of the celebrated De Bériot. It comes down to us of the present day in the familiar names of Vieuxtemps, Léonard, Artot, Monastério, Cœnen, Wéry, Standish, Beumer, Colyns, Prume, Steveniers, the sisters Milanollo, Mademoiselle Fréry, and the sisters Ferni, all distinguished violinists or able professors.

The Guides, or Horse Guards of Belgium, have

long been celebrated for their fine military music; and the orchestra of the Brussels Opera, long under the direction of the clever violinist Singelée (whose daughter, after having appeared with some success as a violinist, afterwards sang in opera as *prima donna* with the celebrated Mademoiselle Titiens and others), was one of the finest in Europe about the middle of this century. It was chiefly composed of young artistes from the *Conservatoire de Bruxelles*.

It was the direction of the violin school of that important institution that, in the full zenith of his powers as a *virtuoso* and a composer, De Bériot was called upon to take. And a good fortune it has been for all those who have left that excellent school to gain their livelihood by musical art, in whatever form.

De Bériot was born at Louvain in 1802. He came of a good family, for his parents were of noble extraction; but he had the misfortune to be left an orphan at the early age of nine years.

He appears to have been left entirely without fortune; for at this tender age he was very kindly taken in hand by M. Tiby, a professor of music in Louvain, who had observed the child's precocious love of the art, and who not only became a tutor, but a second father to him. De Bériot's *First Air Varié* is dedicated to that excellent man.

Under M. Tiby's daily instruction he soon be-

CHARLES AUGUSTE DE BERIOT

came tolerably skilful on the violin. While still very young he was able to play one of Viotti's Concertos in a manner that elicited the unanimous applause of his hearers.

Young De Bériot was a lad of high moral character and contemplative mind, and his whole life at this early period seems to have been bent upon improving his musical education, and striving to attain beauty and perfection in art. Beyond his worthy tutor and friend, he had no model to imitate, and he scarcely knew where to look for further instruction.

At that time the Belgian violin school had turned its attention to an exercise-book called "Jacotot's Method," as being an easy and rapid system for acquiring proficiency in violin playing.

De Bériot when a mere youth purchased this work, in order to see what he could do with it; and afterwards called upon the author to solicit further help.

From the study of this "Method" and a conversation he had with M. Jacotot himself, De Bériot learnt little more than two things, namely, that *perseverance triumphs over all obstacles*, and that, in general, *we are not willing to do all that we are able to do*.

These two precepts appear to have guided this celebrated violinist through life. We have ample evidence of it in his own excellent "Violin School," his numerous compositions, and his charming performances.

In 1821, when he had attained the age of nineteen years, it was decided that he should quit his native town, where so few facilities were afforded him. He was then a handsome youth, with a strongly built frame, slightly above the middle height, fine dark eyes and hair, a rather florid complexion, and a very gentlemanly appearance.

After a short residence at Brussels he found his way to Paris, with a letter of introduction to the illustrious Viotti, then director of music at the Opera. De Bériot's greatest ambition at this time was to be heard by Viotti, and, after playing before him, the old master gave him the following piece of advice, which the young Belgian artiste never forgot :—

"You have a fine style," he said ; "give yourself up to the business of perfecting it. Hear all men of talent, profit by everything, but imitate nothing."

There was at this time in Brussels a violinist named Robbrechts, a former pupil of Viotti, and one of the very last artistes who derived instruction directly from the celebrated Italian.

Andreas Robbrechts was born at Brussels on the 18th December 1797, and made rapid progress under Planken, a professor who, like the late worthy M. Wéry (who succeeded him), formed many excellent pupils. He then entered himself at the

CHARLES AUGUSTE DE BERIOT 77

Conservatoire of Paris in 1814, where he also received some private lessons from Baillot, whilst that institution was closed during the occupation of the capital by the allied armies, just after the battle of Waterloo.

It is on record that Viotti, hearing the young Robbrechts play, was so struck with his magnificent tone and broad style, that he undertook to give him some finishing lessons, with the approbation of Baillot. This was soon arranged, and for several years the two violinists were inseparable. Robbrechts even accompanied Viotti in his journey to London, where they were heard more than once in duets. The fact is, the illustrious Italian had recognised in him the pupil who most closely adhered to his own style of playing, and one of the few who were likely to diffuse it in after years. This was the man who was destined to take in hand the no less celebrated De Bériot.

In 1820 Robbrechts returned to Brussels, where he was appointed first violin solo to King William I. It was shortly after this appointment that De Bériot took lessons from him, and he it was who gave him the letter of introduction to Viotti. The same excellent professor also gave instruction to the young Artot, who afterwards became a most distinguished artiste and a well-known composer of violin music.

Robbrechts died in 1860, the last *direct* representative of the great Viotti school, continued by De Bériot and Artot.

It will now be seen where Charles De Bériot acquired the first principles of that large, bold, and exquisitely charming style that in after-life characterised both his performances and his numerous compositions, and which, in spite of the marked influence of his contemporary Paganini, he retained to the last. I am strongly of opinion, also, that his music will last longer than that of Paganini, and I have been convinced that, in many respects, it is superior to that of the great Italian artiste.

Arriving at Paris, eager for progress, and probably thinking that the classical style of the master he had just left would not lead him on quickly enough or far enough, he sought Viotti himself, with the result which we mentioned above. He then entered himself as a pupil at the Conservatoire of Paris with the view of taking lessons from Baillot.

I have often wondered whether at this period of his life, 1821 to 1824 or thereabouts, De Bériot was in any way influenced by the enormous success of Lafont and Paganini as wandering artistes. It may perhaps be admitted that such was the case; for the reputation of the great Genoese violinist had then begun to spread beyond the boundaries of his native country, and as for Lafont, his name had long been popular throughout Europe.

CHARLES AUGUSTE DE BERIOT 79

However that may be, the young Belgian artiste did not remain more than a few months at the Paris Conservatoire, but applied himself, all the same, most assiduously to the study of his instrument, relying entirely upon his own resources, and seeking aid from no one. Perhaps this was what Viotti meant when he gave him those well-remembered words of advice.

At this time De Bériot possessed a very fine old violin by Paolo Giovanni Magini, a celebrated maker who worked at Brescia, in the Tyrol, where he was born in 1590, and died in 1640. He was a workman and apprentice of the celebrated maker Gasparo da Salo, so named from the little town of Salo, where he made his instruments. The violins of Gasparo and those of Magini are extremely rare and valuable. They have been often imitated by modern makers, and it is not always easy to detect a genuine instrument from a fraudulent imitation, though a good violinist can generally discover the difference by playing upon them.

How De Bériot got this fine old violin it is impossible to say, but that its peculiar plaintive quality and fine tone well suited his playing we can easily believe.

Very soon after this visit to Paris he appeared in several concerts, and always with a brilliant success. Like Paganini, he appeared before the public for the first time in *compositions of his own*, which were, of course, entirely novel. These were some of his first *Airs Variés*, consisting of a dramatic introduction, a simple melodious theme, followed by three or four variations, and a brilliant finale. They won him universal applause by their freshness and originality as much as by his finished execution and large style of cantabile.

In 1826 he went direct to London from Paris, *preceding Paganini by some years*, and met with the same success that had attended his efforts in France. His style was new, his performance most exquisite, and the enthusiasm with which he was everywhere greeted, both in London and the provinces, established for him a lasting reputation.

The circumstance of De Bériot having appeared in England about five years before Paganini must be looked upon as a piece of that good fortune which frequently attends the efforts of earnest, striving men. Had he tarried in his studies and arrived here after the marvellous Italian *virtuoso*, how different the result might have been!

It is not that De Bériot had not wonderful qualities of his own, which would have enabled him to secure success in any country; but no one can doubt that the impression he produced here in London would have been much diminished. In fact, so it happened in 1834, before the influence of Paganini's concerts had calmed down, when a Florentine violinist named Masoni, whose powers of execution were perhaps even greater than those of De Bériot, appeared; but he had been preceded by the great Genoese, and, though under other circumstances his playing would have been considered the most wonderful ever heard, he was obliged to leave for America, and thus Europe lost sight of him altogether.

My father, who was one of the best judges of violin playing that ever lived, often remarked to me that there was a superb tone and a peculiar charm in De Bériot's performance that were probably never possessed by any violinist of this century. During my long residence in Brussels I never heard this great artiste except in the classes—he had ceased to appear in public—so that I cannot judge of him upon the concert platform; but it was universally admitted that even early in his career his playing was characterised by most refined taste, a rich and charming tone, and wonderful execution.

After travelling for several years, and meeting everywhere with the most enthusiastic reception, he returned to Belgium, and had the honour of being presented to King Wilhelm of the Netherlands. This monarch, though exceedingly fond of pictures, knew little or nothing of music; nevertheless, he was a warm patron of art in any form, and he understood that it was necessary to ensure the independence of a young artiste who gave promise of becoming a great ornament to his country. He therefore bestowed upon him a pension of two thousand florins (about £160) per annum, and the title of First Violin Solo to His Majesty.

De Bériot had not long enjoyed this most gratifying position when the Revolution of 1830, which separated Belgium from Holland, broke out, and deprived him of it. It was at this critical period that he formed the acquaintance of the celebrated singer, Madame Malibran, whom he afterwards married. Their friendship arose in Paris in 1830, where she was singing in Italian opera.

The short though glorious career of this gifted singer shines forth like a brilliant meteor in the firmament of art, and her influence upon the great violinist was most marked.

Maria Felicia Garcia, afterwards Madame Malibran, belonged to a family of most distinguished musicians. She was educated by her father, the tenor Garcia, a man of world-wide reputation, and her earliest youth gave evidence of the most surprising talent. At the age of thirteen she was a perfect musician, and at fifteen, when she came with her parents to London, she obtained a complete triumph by performing accidentally in Rossini's *Il Barbiere*, to supply the place of the *prima donna* of the evening, who was unable to appear.

We cannot tarry here to enter into the details of her poetic existence. Her father having taken her to the United States, where she fulfilled a number

CHARLES AUGUSTE DE BERIOT 83

of engagements with increasing success, she finally espoused there a rich merchant named Malibran, a man of French extraction, much older than herself. It was a most ill-advised marriage, and to make matters worse, the merchant failed very soon afterwards. Some go so far as to say that he foresaw this bankruptcy before he contracted his marriage, and hoped to regain his fortune by the proceeds of the eminent singer's career. However that may be, a separation took place, and Madame Malibran returned to Paris in 1827. Her singing in Italian opera was everywhere a source of the most enthusiastic ovation, and as she rose like a star of the first magnitude in the heaven of song, so the young Charles De Bériot was fast earning his laurels as one of the greatest violinists of the day.

In 1830 an indissoluble friendship united these two kindred spirits; and in 1832, De Bériot, Luigi Lablache, the great basso, and Madame Malibran set out for a tour in Italy, where the latter had operatic engagements at Milan, Rome, and Naples, and where all three appeared in concerts, with the most extraordinary success, as may well be imagined. At Bologna, in 1834, it is difficult to say whether the wonderful cantatrice, the charming violinist, or the superb basso produced the greatest sensation; but Madame Malibran's bust was, there and then, placed under the peristyle of the Opera House.

Henceforward De Bériot never quitted her, and their affection seems to have increased as time wore on. In the year following she appeared in London, where she gave forty representations at Drury Lane, performing in *La Sonnambula* of Bellini, the *Maid of Artois* of Balfe, and many other pieces, for which, in this one season, she received the sum of £3200. We imagine this is more than De Bériot, with all his talent, would have made in one season by his violin!

Another journey to Italy, more operatic successes, more concerts, a return to Paris, and finally, in 1836, a proper divorce from the French-American merchant having been obtained, La Malibran and De Bériot were married in due form.

But alas! the joys of this union were destined to be of short duration. After an illness of nine days, the celebrated singer died at Manchester that same year, whither she had gone with her husband to fulfil an engagement.

During these nine fearful days De Bériot only once quitted his wife's bedside, and it was at her special request, to perform at a concert for which he was engaged. When the day arrived she manifested, as she had always done, the greatest anxiety for his success; and when, in reply to her constant inquiries, her friends informed her of the applause that had greeted his performance, a soft angelic

CHARLES AUGUSTE DE BERIOT 85

smile lit up her pale features, which all her suffering could not repress.

The gifted Bellini died at the age of thirty-four, on the 23rd September 1835. The beautiful and exquisite singer Malibran followed him, at the age of twenty-eight, on the 23rd September 1836.

Her premature death is said to have been the result of an accident while riding on horseback in Hyde Park, an exercise of which she was passionately fond, as she was also of dancing; and my father, who knew her for a short time, told me she danced very well, but that her clever conversation and consummate wit were quite equal to her wonderful singing and piano playing. Her sister, Madame Viardot-Garcia, who resembled her in the latter respects, is still living in Paris at the time we are writing (1895).

When all was over, De Bériot, usually so calm and contemplative, became frantic. The adorable mother of his only child was thus taken suddenly away—all his hopes were shattered. In order to secure the fortune of this child—young Charles Vincent De Bériot, for some years a schoolfellow of mine, and afterwards a very distinguished pianist and composer—De Bériot had to fly to Paris before his wife's funeral took place. *No one knew the motives of this sudden disappearance*, and in England he was freely accused of villainy and cruelty. It is scarcely necessary to add that this accusation was most unjust. *The great violinist was the slave of circumstances.*

The funeral service was performed at Manchester on the 1st October 1836, and the remains of the immortal songstress were interred at the Collegiate Church of that town. The following simple inscription marked her temporary resting-place : " Maria Felicia De Bériot, died 23rd Sept. 1836, at the age of 28 years."

Some time afterwards De Bériot obtained permission to remove the mortal remains of his beloved wife to Laeken, near Brussels. Over her tomb in the beautiful churchyard at Laeken stands the magnificent statue by Geefs—the greatest of Flemish sculptors—a *chef-d'œuvre* of art, and a fit memorial to such talent and such beauty.

More than a year elapsed before De Bériot could at all recover from this irreparable loss.

It was on the 15th December 1837 that Malibran's celebrated sister, Pauline Garcia (afterwards Madame Viardot), made her first public appearance, in a concert at Brussels for the benefit of the poor; and on this occasion De Bériot made his first appearance after the death of his wife. King Leopold I., the Queen, the Prince de Ligne, the members of the *Corps Diplomatique*, and many persons of distinction were present on this occasion.

After some other performances equally brilliant,

CHARLES AUGUSTE DE BERIOT 87

Pauline Garcia quitted Belgium for Germany with her mother and De Bériot.

In the summer of 1838 they returned to Brussels, and then proceeded to Paris, where on the 15th December—the anniversary of the great Brussels concert—this great singer and De Bériot appeared at the *Théâtre de la Renaissance* to a crowded and enthusiastic audience. Among other splendid pieces performed on this occasion was a grand duet for voice and violin by Panseron, entitled *Le Songe de Tartini*.

On the 18th April 1840, Pauline Garcia married M. Viardot, the director of the Italian Opera at Paris; and in the following August, De Bériot espoused Mademoiselle Huber, daughter of a magistrate of Vienna. On his return to Brussels he became director of the violin classes at the *Conservatoire Royal de Musique*, devoting his spare time to composition, and to the education of his son. Though occasionally heard in private, De Bériot ceased giving public concerts after entering on these duties. He made many excellent pupils— Lauterbach, Beumer, Standish, Monastério, Mademoiselle Fréry, and several others. Many years before, about 1829, he gave some gratuitous instruction to the young Henri Vieuxtemps, who afterwards became a celebrated violinist.

By his numerous and exceedingly fine compositions De Bériot has made an imperishable name.

His "Violin School" (or *Méthode de Violon*), now published in every language, has smoothed the path of the student who aims at the higher branches of the musical profession. His numerous duets for violin and piano, gradually increasing in difficulty, and founded on the most beautiful operatic selections, are well calculated to animate the beginner, and to cause him to persevere until he can perform the later productions of this talented master.

For artistes he has written his *École Transcendante*, his *Caprices*, his *Études Caractéristiques*, a great number of *Airs Variés*, and ten *Concertos*, besides a number of fantasias and concert pieces. His music is replete with good taste, it is full of expression and grandeur; and for originality no composer for the violin can be compared with him.

During his life in Brussels, as well as in his numerous journeys, he enjoyed the society of the most distinguished men of his day. To his friend the Prince de Chimay, a great patron of art, he owed many opportunities of enchanting the most select of audiences; and one of his finest works is dedicated to the Princess. It is related that it was at the residence of the Prince de Chimay at Ath, in Belgium, that the beautiful Madame Malibran first made known her feelings towards the great violinist (who at that time was much enamoured of Henrietta Sontag). It was after a performance

CHARLES AUGUSTE DE BERIOT 89

of his exquisite *Andante et Rondo Russe* that, according to Countess Merlan, the fair songstress seized his hands, and plainly told him that she adored him.

His splendid *First Concerto* is dedicated to King Leopold I., and his *Ninth Concerto* to the Russian Princess Youssoupoff, whose husband was De Bériot's particular friend, and a distinguished amateur violinist.

Late in life the eminent composer's eyesight began to fail, and the malady increased so much that some time before his death he became totally blind. It was during one of his visits to the residence of his friend Prince Youssoupoff, at St. Petersburg, that his last illness overtook him. He died April 13th, 1870, aged sixty-eight years.

VII

A SOUVENIR OF SIVORI

THE well-known Camillo Sivori, who has recently departed from among us, was another Italian violinist whose name has been popular for many years past in every civilised country. Several notices upon him have appeared in the pages of the musical journals by persons who, perhaps, knew him better than I did, but a few more lines on so eminent an artiste will probably prove acceptable.

In my younger days, at Brussels and Paris, when my time was equally divided between philosophical and medical studies and my violin—between the years 1850 and 1860—there were two great models which guided me as far as music was concerned. The one was Marietta Alboni, the finest singer I ever heard, and the other was Camillo Sivori, the finest violinist.

The performances of these two gifted artistes have been ever since present in my mind. They first initiated me to that purity and breadth of style without which singing and violin playing rarely

A SOUVENIR OF SIVORI

reach above mediocrity; and for the last thirty years the spirit of their music has haunted me like a charm whenever I stepped upon the concert platform to display my own modest efforts in the same direction. It is, undoubtedly, an immense advantage to a young man to have thus placed before him in early life such admirable models, for nothing can aid him more in his arduous striving after perfection.

The late Madame Jullien told me that Sivori made his first appearance in England as a solo player in Jullien's popular concerts. It was reported that he was a pupil of Paganini, and one of the very few persons to whom the celebrated Genoese gave any lessons. She also told me that the violin upon which Sivori played was a Vuillaume, a statement which I could scarcely credit, for the finest Stradivari instrument would barely account for his splendid tone. But I found out afterwards that she was perfectly correct in her statement. I knew Vuillaume personally for a short time in 1856, and I knew some of his violins. Both the man and his ingenious work are deserving of our highest respect, and no doubt the instrument used by Sivori was one of the best ever made in France. When I came to London, about 1861, the violins of Vuillaume, with box and bow included, were being sold here for £14. Many of them now fetch as much as £40 or £50, and even more. It was Sivori himself who told Madame Jullien that his violin was made by Vuillaume. It now stands in the Museum at Genoa, alongside of that used by Paganini (a Guarneri that was given to him by a French amateur violinist named Livron, a merchant residing at Leghorn). It has a dark yellowish varnish, that of Paganini being dark red.

Many years ago an article in the *Quarterly Review* did full justice to the influence exercised by Monsieur Jullien upon music in England. To his praiseworthy efforts the people of Great Britain were indebted for much good music at cheap prices, and for the introduction of many fine performers. Madame Jullien herself was mainly instrumental in enticing to London one of the greatest of modern singers, Mademoiselle Titiens; and her husband introduced to us one of the greatest violinists that ever lived, in the person of Camillo Sivori.

The wonderful career of this celebrated *virtuoso* conveys more than one important lesson. Like the distinguished Norwegian artiste, Ole Bull, he lost his first winnings—quite a comfortable fortune—and had to begin his working life over again, having fallen into some of those speculative traps that ensnare so many successful musicians in America and elsewhere. It is well, indeed, when enough strength and courage remain to enable them to begin again.

In England, Sivori played frequently at the concerts of the Musical Union, directed by the late Professor Ella—a name revered by many of our older musicians—who also introduced Guido Papini to the British public.[1]

At a musical party in London in which Sivori had played and had produced a great sensation, he was addressed by a very indifferent musician, a native of Carlsruhe, in somewhat questionable French, who said—

"Signor Sivori, you are said to be a pupil of Paganini. So am I!"

"Indeed!" exclaimed the other, "this is something new."

"Just so; I will explain. I was very young at the time. It was at Carlsruhe. My father, who played the alto in the orchestra there, said to me one day, 'John, my boy, the great Paganini gives a concert here to-morrow, and I intend that you shall hear him. The price of the places is so high that I cannot get any free tickets, and therefore you must come into the orchestra with me; you will play the triangle, for which you will get your two dollars, and have the advantage of hearing the great man at the same time.'

"Well, at rehearsal, shortly afterwards, I determined to show the celebrated Italian that I was as enthusiastic a musician as he was; so when the

---

[1] See Phipson: "Guido Papini and the Italian School of Violinists." London. 1886. F. W. Chanot, Berners Street, W.

bell comes in the *Rondo de la Clochette*, my little triangle went *ping, ping, ping*, echoing again and again through the empty concert room. Paganini's eyes turned in my direction and flashed fire. ' *Troppo forte! troppo forte!*' he exclaimed.

"We began again; but the second time was no better than the first. The clear *ping* of the triangle rang out so loud that the *harmonic* notes of the violin, which echoed it, or were supposed to echo it, were nowhere!

"Then Paganini, muttering some fearful Italian words, laid down his violin and sprang into the orchestra. I thought he was going to strangle me; but he only seized my triangle, tore it from my hands, and, holding it in the air, gave it three delicate little touches which I shall never forget, making me understand distinctly the exact kind of sound he wished elicited from it. That was my first and *only* lesson from the great Paganini...."

The first time I heard Sivori was at the St. Hubert Theatre at Brussels. All the *élite* of the capital were present, and the dress circle looked particularly gay and animated, the military uniforms of the pupils of the *École Militaire* setting off the elegant toilettes of the ladies, and the white and gold decorations of the house appearing very handsome. The stalls, parquet, and parterre were closely packed. After the performance of a small one-act opera, which gave much pleasure, the cur-

A SOUVENIR OF SIVORI

tain rose upon a plain scene representing a room of moderate dimensions, without any furniture, and in a few moments Signor Sivori stepped from the wings and placed himself in front of the orchestra, near the footlights, and a little to the right of the prompter's box.

He was very cordially received, and made several elegant bows to the audience. Being a man of small stature, his violin appeared to be very much larger than usual: for upon the stage his diminutive height was not very apparent; it was the violin that appeared large, whilst the man appeared of ordinary size.

He played the celebrated *Rondo de la Clochette* of Paganini, and the effect he produced was magical. His tone was magnificent, and I ascribed it at first, erroneously, to the great size of the violin. The beauty of his double notes was peculiar. I had never before heard anything equal to it. When he came to the pizzicato passages a peculiar smile lit up his pale countenance (for he was at heart a classic), which was the more telling as he wore no moustache. His whiskers gave him more the appearance of a respectable Englishman than of a foreigner, and his demeanour was extremely modest and retiring. But there was a sly sparkle in his eyes, which gave a somewhat humorous character to his physiognomy. Nothing could be finer than his rich tone, and his complete mastery over the most intricate passages. The whole performance was easy, graceful, and energetic, without the slightest affectation. The applause at the end of each part was rapturous in the extreme, and at the conclusion he had to come forward and bow several times before the curtain fell.

Until that day I knew nothing but two or three Concertos by De Bériot and two pieces by Artot. The *Rondo de la Clochette* of Paganini, which I thus heard for the first time, was a revelation to me : it revealed at the same time the great resources of the violin as a solo instrument, and its prodigious effect upon the public when in the hands of such a master as Camillo Sivori.

VIII

THE TWO JOSEPHS OF CREMONA

IN these days, when such enormous prices are paid for old Cremona violins, the following considerations may prove interesting, and perhaps useful, to that large section of the British public which devotes most of its time to music and musical instruments. Anything that can throw light upon the history of old Cremona instruments will probably prove the more welcome inasmuch as the sources of information in this respect are becoming daily more scanty and more distant.

Almost all the great connoisseurs of old violins have gone from among us, without leaving their mantle upon the shoulders of their successors. The archives of the old cities of Italy have been ransacked, to a great extent in vain; and hundreds of fine old instruments, which might have served as types or models, have been, and are being, more or less, destroyed by the ruthless hand of time.

The violin has been frequently called "the king of instruments;" but it is often a king without any well-marked line of descent, and one whose pedigree, or genealogy, can only be made out with the greatest of difficulty and much uncertainty. It is true that the shepherd can distinguish the various sheep of his flock one from the other, as an expert botanist can distinguish mosses and grasses, though, to the uninitiated, they are all precisely alike. And so, with regard to violins, there are yet a few persons in the world whose eyes and ears are as keen for those instruments as are the eyes of the shepherd for the woolly-backed creatures of his fold.

During the last thirty years I have had frequent opportunities of studying the instruments of the old Cremona makers, as well as others; and being, not a collector of violins, but a violinist, I am not quite so liable to be prejudiced by mere appearance or hearsay. This cannot be said of many who have been, or still are, afflicted with what may be termed *the collector's craze*, which can only be compared to bibliomania in literary men of morbid tendencies.

One of the greatest violinists that ever lived, Nicolo Paganini, of Genoa, happened to play upon a violin made by a workman of Cremona, named Giuseppe Antonio Guarneri (or Guarnerius, for they had the habit of Latinising names of distinguished men in those days), which he had given to him under peculiar circumstances[1] by a wealthy French dilettante residing in Italy.

[1] See Phipson: "Biographical Sketches and Anecdotes of Celebrated Violinists." London: R. Bentley & Son. 1877.

THE TWO JOSEPHS OF CREMONA 99

Until that fact became known to the public, the violins most in vogue for sweetness and power were those of the celebrated Nicolo Amati, and the no less celebrated Antonio Stradivari, his workman. In Great Britain, Richard Duke, of London, was at that time (latter end of eighteenth and beginning of nineteenth centuries) considered the best maker; and he was quite fashionable among the rich amateurs of the West End. But even in those early days it had been long held, not only in England, but throughout the whole of Europe, that the violins of the Tyrol and of Cremona were the finest in the world. The instruments made by members of the Amati family brought the largest prices in the market all through the seventeenth and eighteenth centuries. Then came Stradivari, in many respects a most remarkable man, who actually superseded his master, Nicolo Amati, and was ranked during the eighteenth century as now, the maker of the finest violins and violoncellos ever produced.

The only makers who ever quite equalled Stradivari were, in the first instance, Lorenzo Guadagnini, who was his workman for thirty-five years, and who manufactured violins, on his own account, for about five years after the death of his celebrated master. He used to label his instruments thus: "*Lorenzo Guadagnini da Cremona, alumnus Stradiuarius.*" All his violins nowadays, and for some time past, are, and have been, sold as Stradivarius instruments, from which it is almost impossible to distinguish them, and the name "Stradivarius" is a talisman in the market.

Next came Giuseppe Antonio Guarneri, who occasionally made violins equal in sweetness and power to those of Stradivari; and the same may be said, with the greatest probability, as regards the work of Carlo Bergonzi (another workman in the shop of Stradivari), Lupot (formerly of Stuttgard, then of Lyons), Médard, and a few others, such as Sebastian Kloz, of Mittenwald in the Tyrol, one of whose violins was sold in London for £300 about forty years ago.

Stradivarius, as the English connoisseurs generally call him, worked till he was over ninety years of age, and turned out a very large number of violins and violoncellos. Probably at the lowest estimate, some seven thousand instruments—violins, tenors, and 'cellos—must have left the celebrated Cremona workshop during the long life of that extraordinary man. The latest example of his market value is evinced in the sale of the Stradivarius violin that used to belong to the late M. Alard (head of the French Conservatoire violin classes, and son-in-law of Vuillaume the violin-maker). It was bought for £2000, a year or two ago, by Mr. Crawfurd, a Yorkshire gentleman. His usual price for a violin was about £4 English money, unless specially ornamented or made to

THE TWO JOSEPHS OF CREMONA 101

order for some nobleman. An uninjured instrument of Stradivarius will, at present, fetch in a public auction room from £200 to £800, or even £1000. This latter sum was realised in 1888.

A few violins made by Giuseppe Antonio Guarneri, usually called "Joseph Guarnerius," have realised as much as £400 to £700 in public auction. Of course there is a good deal of fancy, prejudice, or "craze" in all this; for there are thousands of people that frequent the concert room who could not distinguish between the sound of a violin that cost £500 or £1000 and one that cost only £25, or even less, provided it was played by a genuine artiste.

During the seventeenth and eighteenth centuries there were a considerable number of clever makers of violins in the ancient city of Cremona, whose sons, nephews, and workmen spread to Milan, Mantua, Venice, Rome, and Naples. Some also went to Paris, Stuttgart, Nancy, and to the Tyrol, whence the great Cremona makers originally came; so that the talent of violin construction spread far and wide over Europe.

Nevertheless, it is rather surprising how seldom an instrument made by any except those who have been termed the "great masters" ever gives perfect satisfaction either to the player or to the audience. The tone of a Stradivarius violin in good condition is round and full, deliciously sweet, yet powerful, quite devoid of the nasal or hurdy-gurdy quality, and possessing such equality that the four strings are as one—that is, there is no perceptible difference in quality when the bow of the player passes from one string to the other.

When it became widely known that the celebrated Paganini usually played upon a Guarnerius violin, the instruments of that maker came rapidly into vogue. They were not only very much sought after by amateurs, but have been extensively imitated by many modern makers, especially since 1840 or thereabouts. It would seem that many performers fancied that everything depended on the *maker* of the violin whether they could hope to play like Paganini or not! This maker died in Cremona, in 1745, at the age of sixty-two. He made many violins of a small pattern. Those of the larger pattern, which are the most esteemed, are extremely rare; but they have been much imitated by later makers. This was not a difficult thing to do, as the workmanship is rather rough and careless, and the sound-holes of a peculiar, ugly shape. Violinists, both amateur and professional, were all anxious to possess a real "Joseph Guarnerius," and the singular craze continues to this day.

But there was another Joseph Guarnerius at Cremona, a cousin or an uncle of the one first alluded to, dating much further back. Some say he lived

THE TWO JOSEPHS OF CREMONA 103

from 1690 to 1730, and others that his span of life was 1680 to 1710; so he must have died when he was thirty or forty years of age. He also was a good violin maker, but very little is known about him, though he is supposed to have taught his art to the younger Joseph.

The violins of this other Joseph Guarnerius (usually denominated as the "son of Andreas Guarnerius") now fetch in the market as much as £150 or more, according to their quality and state of preservation. But they are very seldom met with, and not at all known even by men who have the reputation of being experts. They are much more scarce than the violins of Stradivarius and Amati; and these are quite rare enough! But when the rage broke out among artistes and amateurs for having a "Guarnerius violin" like that of Paganini, when all the instruments of Joseph Guarnerius the younger had been bought up long ago, some dealers in Paris made a little play with the other Joseph—*Giuseppe, figlio d'Andrea* (Joseph, son of Andreas), as he was, and is still, called—and a few of these violins found their way into the hands of wealthy amateurs in this country about 1840.

In the little workshop of Nicolo Amati in Cremona—the most famous violin maker of his day—besides the workman Antonio Stradivari, the best, and afterwards the most celebrated violin maker that ever lived (though let us not hide the fact that several others have been known to equal him)—there was another workman, called Andrea Guarneri, whose name was also destined to become popular, thanks to the extraordinary artistic career of Paganini, and the fact that he played on a Guarneri violin. This man Andrea also set up for himself, at a shop in Cremona dedicated to *Santa Teresa*, and made a number of instruments which partake much of the Amati pattern and quality. But he had a peculiar way of cutting the sound-holes, by which his violins can often be recognised at once: he made the lower circle of the hole much larger than it had ever been made before. This feature has been imitated by later makers, but the imitators have neglected to supply the other characteristics of the old sound-hole of the original Brescian school.

This Andrea Guarneri (or Andreas Guarnerius, as he is called in England) purchased at the time he set up his own workshop a fine piece of pine wood, noted for its sonorous qualities, from which he and his son made the tables of all their violins. Hence the violins of these makers have a peculiarity due to this circumstance: they exhibit a dark stain, more or less intense, and especially visible when the violin is held away from the light—for instance, when the observer stands with his back to the window, and holds the instrument horizontally before him. This stain extends on either side of the finger board, along the whole length of the table, and is

THE TWO JOSEPHS OF CREMONA 105

rather less than a quarter of an inch in width, often very faint except in the central portion. It is due to the wood in these parts being rather more impregnated with turpentine resin. This feature, which cannot be imitated, is found in all the genuine Guarnerius violins, and will almost invariably help us to distinguish a genuine Guarnerius violin from a spurious imitation. The violins of the elder Joseph have been hitherto little if at all imitated by other makers, as they are so little known, whilst imitations of the younger Joseph have been made by thousands.

Charles Reade, the novelist, was an enthusiastic collector of and dealer in violins, and he assured us that, with very few exceptions (notably George Chanot, who died the other day), all the connoisseurs of old violins had died out, and that to distinguish instruments of different makers as the shepherd does the sheep of his flock is now a lost art. We quite agree with him. The poor Milanese *bric-a-brac* violin hunter, Luigi Tarisio, to whom modern makers, such as the late M. Vuillaume of Paris, and others, owed so much of their knowledge, carried the art with him to the grave in 1853. A violin by Joseph Guarnerius, *fil. Andræ*, which was purchased in Paris by Charles Reade for about £24, was put into public auction in London without a name, and fetched £120.

With respect to quality, an experienced player should be able to judge of that without much difficulty. With amateurs, in nine cases out of ten, it is not so much defects in an instrument as want of practice in the player that causes fault to be found with the quality of a violin. No doubt there do exist many wretched instruments in the world—trash that ought to be burned forthwith, and not used even in a large orchestra; but as regards solo playing, it matters little to an artiste, as far as the public is concerned, whether he plays on a violin that cost £40 or £400. It would require a very delicate ear to detect any difference, unless the two instruments were played immediately one after the other. All we can say is that the player who possesses a violin of the value of £400 will generally please his audience more in the cantabile passages than one who plays upon an instrument worth only one-tenth of the money. Moreover, a great deal depends upon the execution; for a clever violinist will make his effect with an instrument which, in the hands of an indifferent player, would be quite displeasing, or disagreeable to listen to.

The family of the Guarneri, in Cremona, consisted of the father Andrea, his brother Pietro, his son Giuseppe—who had a son also called Pietro—and his nephew Giuseppe Antonio, son of a cloth merchant, and often called "Giuseppe del Gesu." In their days Italian tradesmen had the habit of naming their shops after some patron saint. That of the Guarneri family was Saint Theresa; hence

THE TWO JOSEPHS OF CREMONA 107

the name *Santa Teresa* is found on their labels. They often belonged to religious sects, and *Giuseppe del Gesu* is so called nowadays in Italy because he invariably placed after his name on the labels of his violins the initials I.H.S., with a cross over or through the H. This evidently indicated that he belonged to a Society of Jesuits. There is a considerable difference between the violins of the two Josephs. The instruments of Giuseppe Antonio are usually rough in appearance, having much less careful finish than those of other Cremona makers, and acute, ugly sound-holes. It is only by playing upon them, and thus appreciating their splendidly brilliant tone, that the maker of these violins is at once revealed. They are brilliant, round, and sweet upon the three strings, but the G, or fourth string, is of a dry quality, and less round in tone than in the Stradivari or Amati violins. This character is notable in all the violins of the Guarneri family, and least so, as far as my experience goes, in the violins of the elder Joseph. The violins of the latter are less flat in model, without, however, being so elevated as the Amati or Stainer instruments, and their varnish, of a rich golden yellow, is extremely fine. Charles Reade called this Guarnerius "the king of varnishers." It sets off the wood of the back and sides to great advantage. In these Guarneri violins the middle bouts are narrowed under the shoulders, but spread out rapidly towards the lower extremity, which gives the instrument a peculiarly elegant appearance. When the back is of two pieces, the pattern or grain of the wood is turned upwards, instead of downwards as with most other makers. On the table, on each side of the finger board, are invariably seen the two dark stains to which I have already alluded. The lower aperture of the sound-holes is much larger than usual, and the peg-holes in the scroll are also much larger, and take thicker pegs than are required by violins of any other makers.

All these details of form and structure, combined with the fine tone of the instrument, will enable our readers to distinguish a genuine Guarneri violin from any others, for I have insisted here upon the absolutely distinctive characters of these instruments, several of which are neglected by the cleverest imitators, or cannot be imitated. This knowledge, which has accumulated, year by year, since I was a boy in Brussels more than forty years ago, has enabled me often to save my friends from imposture; for the rage to possess a "Guarnerius violin" is almost as great now as it ever was. But to show how little they are known to those who profess to be experts, I will relate a little anecdote. Some ten or twelve years ago, when real judges of violins were becoming already very rare, I took a beautiful Guarnerius to three noted dealers in London, one after the other, on the same day, and

THE TWO JOSEPHS OF CREMONA 109

each one gave a different opinion. Not one of them recognised it as a Guarnerius, though it came originally from the great Tarisio for the sum of £100, and at the present day is worth five times that amount!

IX

A VIOLIN RECITAL IN MONGOLIA

I HAVE often been amused by hearing a fine violin spoken of as a "fiddle," knowing how very much more ancient is the latter instrument, and that the former is not even derived from it. In fact, there is not the slightest connection between the two. It is true that the term "fiddle" is often applied sarcastically to denote a *bad violin*, and it is commonly used by many who ought to be aware of the different origins of these two instruments, but appear, on the contrary, to be totally ignorant of it. I do not deny that they may both have had a common origin, in the same way that all men are supposed to have come down from Adam; so that the *fiddle* used in the tenth century at the fairs and merry-makings of the Anglo-Saxons, an instrument which is believed by some learned antiquarians to have originated in England, or Wales, and the Amati violin of many hundred years later, may probably be looked upon as modern representatives of some of those very ancient, queer-looking stringed instruments cut upon the stone of old Egyptian and

A VIOLIN RECITAL IN MONGOLIA 111

Grecian monuments, or of the "long pattern" monochords which have existed in India from what might rightly be termed pre-historic times, and were certainly caused to sound by means of a bow.

The violin—*violino*, or small *viola*—was directly derived from the *viola d'amore*, in that essentially musical district the Tyrol and Northern Italy. Thanks to the writings and performances of Mr. Henry Saint George, the *viola d'amore* may again become the vogue in our modern concerts and drawing-rooms. Although this transformation of the *viola d'amore* (or *viola da gamba*) into the *violino*, or modern violin, took place more than three hundred years ago, yet in the East people still make musical instruments that recall the ancient Indian productions. I read some years ago, in a book written by Dr. Hogg, that the admirers of Paganini and performances on one string, would perhaps be surprised to learn that a species of fiddle with a single string is not only well known in Egypt, but is often played in the streets, and, says this writer, "many listen with delight to the melodious sounds drawn from this single string by some wild, untutored Arab." Certainly we were surprised when we read this. A "solo on one string" is not exactly what we should expect to hear in the streets of Cairo. But let us take a slight musical excursion into the deserts of Mongolia, if only to prove, once more, that the love of harmony and the tendency to unite the tones of stringed instruments to the human voice are innate in mankind throughout the world.

In a recent work entitled "Among the Mongols," the Rev. James Gilmour, M.A., a member of the London Mission to Peking, has described the incidents of his life in a portion of the globe rarely visited by representatives of Western civilisation.

At the time of one of his visits to a Mongolian "village"—a small agglomeration consisting of a few coarse tents, a number of savage dogs, some cattle and beasts of burden, and store-boxes—there had been a wedding. Long after that imposing ceremony was over, visiting from tent to tent and feasting were kept up among the Mongolians.

One afternoon, after some conversation with these people, Mr. Gilmour espied a curious-looking instrument lying on the top of one of the store-boxes, and a *lama*, or chief man of the tribe, volunteered to extract music from it.

This instrument is described as a "home-made fiddle." The main parts of it consisted of a hollow box about a foot square and *two or three inches deep*, covered with a sheep's skin; and a stick about three feet long was thrust through the sides of the box.

Here we have the *flat model* of Stradivarius, with the *Cremona varnish* replaced by a sheep's skin!

The instrument had only *two* strings (here we have the *treble* and the *bass*—we can have no more

A VIOLIN RECITAL IN MONGOLIA 113

in a full orchestra !), and these, we are told, consisted of a few hairs pulled from a horse's tail, and lengthened at both ends by pieces of common string (the foreshadowing of the covered 4th, as it will appear some day in Mongolia !).

The bow consisted of a bent whittled branch of some shrub, fitted with a few horse hairs tied on quite loosely (a counterpart of the bow used by the immortal Corelli !). The necessary tension of this bow was produced by the hand of the performer as he grasped it to play.

The missionary found it impossible not to laugh at the sight of so uncouth an instrument. Impolite and disrespectful as this conduct was, the worthy lama to whom the instrument belonged was not in the least disconcerted. Doubtless he was quite used to it. With a smile on his placid countenance, he took up the bow we have described, set the box or body of the fiddle on his knee, and went through the preliminaries of tuning "with all the gravity of an accomplished musician." He then produced from his pocket a small paper of powdered rosin, applied the minutest quantity of this to the hair of the bow, and "subsiding into a permanent attitude, proceeded to entertain his guests with the well-known Mongolian air called *Pinglang Yah.*"

The strains of the instrument, says the rev. gentleman, "were soft and low, and pleasing in the extreme." Compared with the high screeching tones

H

of many Chinese and Mongol instruments, the sound of this one was "more like that of a good piano touched by a skilful hand."

The lama, it appears, was a clever performer; he had made the instrument himself, and knew how to use it. He soon showed his listeners that highly artistic effects could be produced from this very queer fiddle. After he had played a few verses of the song just named, it became evident that "it was time to stop him," says our author; but in what this evidence consisted, we are not informed.

There was a young woman in the tent, the daughter of the lama; she was "clad only in two garments of common rough Chinese cloth, but graceful and beautiful in build and feature. She was just reaching womanhood, and her mouth was adorned by a set of milk-white and perfect teeth. From the looks of the mother it was evident that she wished her daughter to be asked to sing." After a little persuasion she consented, whilst the lama scraped away on his *two* strings (a decided advantage over Paganini's *one* string), and "a very lively concert was the result."

The burden of the song was the praise of a maiden named *Ping Lang*, and the words are supposed to proceed from the mouth of a disappointed suitor, who is stricken with grief when the girl finally mounts her horse and rides off in a procession to become the wife of a more fortunate rival.

A VIOLIN RECITAL IN MONGOLIA

It was rather difficult, we are told, to start the singers, for the artistic lama joined in with his voice; but when once they had begun, it was found to be far more difficult to stop them. We are not informed how this was effected; nor whether, had they not been stopped in some way or other, they would have continued the song for any given length of time. In London or Paris, we know, a violin recital may last a couple of hours at longest; but in Mongolia, where time is less valuable, these entertainments may perhaps continue for the greater part of the day and night, or until the performers drop down from fatigue, like the riders in a twenty-four hours' bicycle race.

At the conclusion, the mother appears to have been highly delighted at the praise which was bestowed upon her daughter; and it seems evident that the good looks of the latter had as much to do with this as the nature of the musical composition. Altogether it appears to have been a most delightful and instructive violin recital, with one vocalist (a second joining in), and would certainly have interested many of the fashionable dilettanti who frequent our London concerts during the season.

And then, we must remember that Mongolia, with its two and a half millions of inhabitants, spread over one and a half millions of square miles, is mostly a desert, comprising part of the vast sandy plain of Gobi, interspersed by a few fertile tracts, feeding large herds of cattle belonging to wandering tribes, and having only three months of summer and nine of winter, which prejudiced foreigners assert is the case with us in England; but Mongolia is much colder. Its vast solitudes are enlivened sometimes by fairs and marriages, and on such occasions we may hear the strains of a "home-made fiddle," whilst Londoners are contenting themselves with those of Joachim or Sarasate. As the religion is Buddhist, there can be little doubt that the art of constructing this stringed instrument came down to the modern Mongols with their religion, from the most remote periods of Indian history.

X

VIOLINS OF VALUE

IT is a charming thing, no doubt, to possess a Nicolo Amati, a Stradivari, or a Guarneri violin in good condition—that is, which has not been accidentally injured or purposely tampered with. Many old Cremona violins have been scraped or patched, or have had certain internal additions made to them, with the view of making them, as it was imagined, more fitted to the strain of the modern pitch. Such instruments are more or less destroyed, and are, of course, less valuable than a good violin by any maker of repute. Those which have not been thus injured realise what are justly termed "fancy prices," fetching anything between £100 and £1000, or even more, according to their quality and state of preservation. Some of the Tyrolean violins, such as those of Sebastian Kloz, are quite equal to any produced in Cremona, but they are far more scarce than the latter.

These fine old violins are not only sought after by *virtuosi*, but, unfortunately, by collectors of *bric-a-brac*; men who attribute the most marvellous properties to varnish, and talk about the "old Cremona varnish" as *a lost art*, and that sort of thing; men who, like the late Joseph Gillott, know nothing of music. His collection of Cremona instruments, when sold by auction in April 1872, realised £4195. No doubt it cost the Birmingham pen-maker more than twice as much. Many of the instruments were really fine, but more were of small value, either on account of having been injured, or because they were spurious, or doubtful as to the maker. Of course the labels inside were all there, but many of them were a very queer mixture of bad Latin, German, or Italian, and anything but genuine. Nowadays no one looks at a label. The time has gone by when an uninitiated purchaser could be imposed upon in this manner. It has become generally known that a label, looking as if it were two hundred years old, can be manufactured without much difficulty.

It is a pity for the musical profession that *bric-a-brac* hunters do not stop at crockery and dusty old books. At the present day there are lying hidden away in boxes scores of fine old violins that could be put to good use in the concert room, and delight the ears of the most enlightened audiences.

Nevertheless, our young artistes need not despair. Although nothing can equal the soft, luscious tone of a well-preserved Stradivari, a violin must be very bad that will not, in the hands of a good player,

VIOLINS OF VALUE 119

make its due effect in a large concert room, even if not quite so pleasant as a Cremona in the drawing-room; and if an artiste can manage to go to about £40, or even less, he may get an instrument with which he can do himself ample justice and make his living.

One day the well-known Charles Dancla was offered the loan of a fine Stradivari violin for one of his concerts; he tried it for ten days, but preferred to play upon his own instrument, that was not worth one-tenth of the money which the other had cost.

Not long ago I was at F. W. Chanot's, in Berners Street, and saw there a magnificent violin made by Maucotel, of London, who died some years ago. Prejudice aside, this instrument would compare well with the finest Cremona ever made, and yet a very moderate price was asked for it. Lucky indeed is the man who purchased it. Its tone was superb, and its appearance equally grand. Maucotel and the late George Chanot worked together in London, and have made good names in the violin world. I also remember a fine violin made by Withers, of London, which in a concert room could not have been distinguished from the best of Cremona instruments. This one was sold to an amateur for £60, and was certainly well worth the money, when we consider what men will give for a Stradivari or a Guarneri, a Guadagnini or a Bergonzi.

And this curious affection for old Cremona violins, tenors, and basses is by no means a modern fancy. The Stradivari violin which my excellent father gave me when I was sixteen years of age was priced one hundred guineas in 1824. But to go still further back, we were told by the English newspapers that in September 1873 there was sold by auction at Dresden the famous violin of Count Trautmansdorf, Grand Equerry to the Emperor Charles VI., which he had purchased direct from the celebrated Tyrolean maker, Jacob Stainer. " He paid him down in cash seventy golden crowns, and undertook to provide the vendor, as long as he lived, with a good dinner every day, as well as a hundred florins a month in cash, and every year a new coat, with golden brandenburghs, two casks of beer, lighting and fuel, and, in case he should marry, as many hares as he might require, with twelve baskets of fruit annually for himself, and as many for his old nurse (housekeeper ?)." As Stainer lived sixteen years afterwards, this violin must have cost the Count not less than 20,000 florins. At the auction in question it was knocked down to a Russian gentleman for 2500 thalers.

Little is known with certainty regarding the life of Jacob Stainer, except that he visited Cremona and nearly married a daughter of Nicolo Amati, returned to the Tyrol, where he worked with

Kloz and Albani, experienced great vicissitudes of fortune, and finally, after the death of his German wife, retired to a monastery, where he made a few magnificent violins.[1] So that the above story may well be looked upon with a sceptical eye—as a story concocted, perhaps, for the auction room, like those queer rumours that sometimes float about on the Stock Exchange.

It is only during the last forty years or so that Cremona violins have sold freely at more than a hundred guineas, which was the price usually put upon them about the middle of the present century. Of late years one of the highest figures we meet with was that realised by a Stradivari violin that belonged to the old maker, John Betts, of London. It bears the date 1704, and was purchased by the late George Hart, of Princes Street, Leicester Square, for £800, in 1878. Old John Betts bought it for a sovereign over his shop counter (near the Royal Exchange) some seventy years previously.

That same year, 1878, in February, we read in *Galignani's Messenger*, an English newspaper long published in Paris, that a Stradivari violin, signed and dated 1709, was sold by auction at the Hôtel Druot. It was put up at 10,000 francs (£400), and finally bought for 22,100 francs (£884). During this sale, when the bidding had gone up

[1] The best account of Jacobus Stainer's life is to be found in Fleming's "Old Violins and their Makers," London 1883.

to 18,000 francs, there was a great rush of the curious to get a sight of it, and a small table, upon which three or four persons were standing, was upset, and they fell to the ground, creating some stir among the crowd. "Do not be alarmed, gentlemen!" exclaimed the auctioneer; "the violin is quite safe."

Violins of value exist, which may not be so from an artiste's point of view. I have seen in the hands of the late eccentric Dr. Forster, of Brussels, and his no less eccentric friend, the Prince de Vismes et de Ponthieu, instruments that a *virtuoso* could scarcely play upon, and which were valued at several hundreds of pounds. My worthy master, Henri Standish, took the first prize at the Brussels Conservatoire (and became afterwards *répétiteur* to De Bériot's class) with an Eggita-Kloz violin that cost 300 francs (£12) in 1849. With this excellent instrument he played in concerts, and made a musical tour with De Bériot.

It sometimes happens that violins of great historical value disappear, apparently for ever, as the famous Elector-Stainer instruments[1] have done. What, for instance, has become of Tom Cooke's violin—that which, amid roars of laughter, he handed up to the judge in the celebrated trial concerning the copyright of a song called *The Old*

---

[1] Those made by Stainer after he entered on a monastic life, and presented to each of the Electors.

VIOLINS OF VALUE

English Gentleman? When the witty leader of the Drury Lane orchestra was called as a witness, and requested to sing the air, he said he could not sing it, but that he could play it on his violin. "Let the violin be brought in," said the judge; and when the airs of the two songs in dispute were played and found to be perfectly identical, the learned judge, struck with their similarity, and turning to the counsel, exclaimed, "*That is a very simple matter,*" alluding, of course, to the legal question. "It is, my lord," put in Tom Cooke, handing up the violin; "*would your lordship like to try it?*"

It is a curious thing that the art of violin-making should have so completely disappeared from the old city of Cremona; but as Signor Frederico Sacchi, a Cremonese gentleman residing in London, has remarked, "it is more than a century since the death of Stradivari's best pupils and imitators, and even the few modern representatives of the traditions of that school, the Cerutis, who exhibited their violins in the great Exhibition of 1851, have joined the majority." But while violin-making has gradually become an art of the past, other industries have arisen there, such as spinning and carding silk, and the preparation of fruit preserves and confectionery.

XI

THE STRADIUARIUS—A DIALOGUE

"You know my fine violin, Bertha?"

"Yes—you mean your Cremona, I suppose—well, what about it?"

"I have made such a discovery! The other day I looked into the inside to see whether I could still make out the inscription on the old label, *Stradiuarius fecit Cremona, &c.*, which is almost obliterated with dust and rosin, and, to my utter surprise, I found, high up above it, and very much to the left, in fact nearly under the finger board (where it was extremely difficult to see it), some writing in very small but distinct characters, though faint, and these were evidently in German. It struck me at once that the violin must have been opened for repairs, and that something had been recorded which, from my ignorance of the German language, I was not able to make out."

"How very odd, George, for that violin has been in our family for a very great number of years, and I never heard of it having been repaired."

"True, my sister, long before you and I were

born, when our dear father was a mere boy, he brought it back with him to England when he returned after his foreign course of study. So you see we have had it since the beginning of the century; it was purchased for him in 1819, four years after the battle of Waterloo, by his music-master, who had served with the Prussians in that campaign. I have a memorandum to that effect in one of my father's diaries under the date November 14th, 1819."

"And what a splendid instrument it is, George! I never hear anything like it; still I think a great deal may be owing to your fine playing. Only last week, when Mr. Oldtim came to tune our piano, he heard you, and said he thought it had an exquisitely sweet and powerful tone, and he is a good judge, you know — but what do you mean by your *discovery?*"

"Last year, you remember, I refused an offer of £500 for this violin, because the tone, as you say, is so fine, and the double notes are so beautiful, whilst the harmonics are so round and clear. And I have often thought that the possession of a fine Cremona violin is the greatest luxury in the world to a musician. Such violins are, of course, extremely rare. Besides all this, it is easy to play, the tone is smooth and equal on all the four strings; it is like a splendid mezzo-soprano voice. Then when the old label, *Stradiuarius fecit Cremona, anno 1717,* happens to catch my eye, I cannot help thinking what an admirable workman he must have been, and what a debt of gratitude all violinists owe to him, and his conscientious fellow-labourers, his two sons, and Lorenzo Guadagnini, who helped him.

"You see there were once at Cremona, in the same workshop, near the old church of Santo Domenico, three men named Nicolo Amati, Andrea Guarneri, and Antonio Stradivari, who have left three of the greatest reputations in the world of musical instrument makers, men who have supplied musicians with some of the finest-toned violins ever heard."

"Oh yes, George, I have often heard of them, and of the enormous prices some rich enthusiasts have given for their instruments. Yet you once told me that Stradivari never got more than about 100 francs, or £4, for any violin he made, unless it was specially ornamented to suit the taste of the purchaser."

"It is so, my dear sister. In the eighteenth century there was but one price for a first-rate violin all over Europe; it was about fifty shillings of our English money, and a violin of Cremona, being rather more sought after, went up to something higher, and in the case of Stradivarius to as much as £4. These violins now sell at £200 to £2000, when in good condition and well preserved."

THE STRADIUARIUS

"It is truly wonderful!"

"Yes; but what is more wonderful still has been revealed to me within the last fortnight by the old writing I discovered inside my violin. This writing has been there, Heaven only knows how long, and is very small and faint. After endeavouring in vain to make it out, with the aid of spectacles and a magnifying glass, I determined to have the instrument opened, for I found that the four lines of inscription had been placed in such a manner that it was quite impossible to read them without taking the violin to pieces in this manner."

"Would not that be a great risk, George?"

"I knew it was a risky thing to do; it is certainly an operation that requires the greatest care, lest the table of the instrument should get cracked as it is being raised, and the violin irretrievably injured. But my curiosity was so great, I could not resist the temptation. So I took it down to William Techler, who is a careful workman and a good German scholar. I waited with him for hours whilst he did it; and when the table was entirely removed we made out the writing, and he translated it for me. Oh, what a revelation it was!"

"Indeed!"

"There were four lines in a small, clear hand, lines which at first looked like the verse of a poem, written with extreme neatness, and in minute German characters."

"And what was the meaning of it, my dear brother?"

"Well, here is the translation on this bit of paper, as I wrote it down from Techler's dictation: 'This instrument is made by G. R., violin-maker at Erfurt, in the year 1786, strictly upon the model of A. S., Cremona.'"

"Oh, my dear George, how very extraordinary."

"Techler tells me that A. S. certainly stands for *Antonio Stradivari*, already at that date celebrated throughout Europe; and one of his violins was, if possible, always procured, or borrowed, by German makers as a model to work upon."

"Only just fancy! And this is a violin equal to any Stradivarius that was ever made!"

"Yes, Bertha; and I have no doubt that hundreds of fine violins have been made in Germany by excellent conscientious workmen, who spared no pains to make their work as perfect as possible, though barely able to subsist by it. And what is more, hundreds of these superior instruments are now sold in Europe and America as 'Cremona violins,' at enormous prices. I tell you the Cremona craze is pure madness. I wonder whether Walker will renew his offer of £500 for it. Shall I give him the opportunity?"

"Oh, George, how can you think of such a thing! No, my dear brother, never part with that violin; you could never replace it. Whoever the

THE STRADIUARIUS

maker may have been, the magnificent tone is there—what more can you desire? Do not be carried away by vulgar prejudice, and so become the victim of the monopoly of a name! A rose by any other name—I mean, my dear brother, a violin without any name may sound as sweet, in *your* hands."

Note.—The above little episode is strictly true. On more than one occasion this interesting instrument has been in my hands. Its tone is very fine, but not quite equal to that of a well-preserved Stradivarius; it is, however, superior to that of some very good instruments with which it was carefully compared. At the present day it is over a hundred years old. The back and table are *both* of one piece; the purfling is perfect, just like that of Stradivari; the model very flat, like that of Sebastian Kloz (which is flatter than that of Stradivari); the varnish, amber yellow, of mediocre quality; the sides slightly narrow, like those of Nicolo Amati, but very handsome; the scroll very fine, and the finish throughout is tolerably perfect. The sound-hole is stiffer than that of Stradivari, and the wood is not equal to that of the finer Cremona violins; but time and much use have mellowed it. There is not a single imperfect note from one end to the other of the scale, in whatever position it may be stopped; and this violin yields the "third sound" with ease when double notes are played, giving to them a very fine quality of tone. What more could be asked of Cremona itself?

XII

OLAUS BULL AND NORWEGIAN POETRY

NORWAY has supplied us with several great artistes, such as Ole Bull, Norman Neruda, Willy Burmester, among violinists, and Marcus Larsen among painters.

I gave in my "Celebrated Violinists" the following quotation from Mr. Rae's clever volume, "The Land of the North Wind." Whilst sailing along the coast of Norway, he anchored at Bodö. "At Bodö," he says, "there came on board a minstrel—though that word, when applied to him, is mere foolishness. He was a collection of minstrels—a band—a *Norwegian musical festival.* With his mouth he played the Pandean pipes, attached round his neck by a scarf; with his right hand he turned a barrel-organ; with his left he played a pair of castanets; his left foot moved a cord which ran under his arm and put a drum-stick in motion—on his back was slung a drum; with his right knee he manœuvred a pair of cymbals hanging from the organ; to his hat was attached a rod, which struck a triangle when he nodded his head; and somewhere about him was a tambourine. When we saw him we were struck with a great awe, and felt that this man was no ordinary being. Was this the familiar god Pan? Was this the genius of Music turned loose upon the earth? Was this Orphée *aux Enfers?* We looked at him, speaking in hushed whispers, and waiting for his first note. When he began to play, all doubt was laid aside: he was Orphée, and we were *aux Enfers!*"

Olaus Bull, or Ole Bull, as he was generally called, was not perhaps quite equal to this ; he was not a complete "Norwegian musical festival," but he used to elicit some astonishment by performing what he called a *quartett on one violin.*

The life of this celebrated violinist has been one of extraordinary adventure. He was born, like the celebrated Holberg of the seventeenth and eighteenth centuries, in the old town of Bergen, on the 5th February 1810. His parents belonged to the leading families of that northern resort of merchants, skippers, timber-dealers, and herring-fishers. His grandmother on his father's side was sister to the well-known poet Edward Storm, the author of the "Sinclair Lay," an epic poem on the Scottish colonel, Sinclair, who, during the rivalry of Gustavus Adolphus and Christian IV., at the commencement of the seventeenth century, made a descent on Norway with a thousand volunteers, three hundred of whom were killed, together with his lovely and courageous wife, by the ferocious Norwegian peasants, who hurled rocks upon them in the pass known as the Guldsbrandsdahl, not very far from Christiania, a valley since become universally admired in the celebrated picture by the Swedish court painter, Marcus Larsen.[1] His father, John Storm Bull, was a pupil of Professor Tromsdorff, the distinguished chemist. His mother had four brothers, two of whom were captains in the army, one a captain in the navy, and one a merchant, who afterwards became the editor of the only newspaper printed in Bergen.

All the members of the family were exceedingly fond of music, and the editor just mentioned had occasional quartett parties at his house, sometimes as often as twice a week, when the works of Haydn, Mozart, and Beethoven were, more or less, executed. Generally speaking, these musical evenings coincided with a dinner party, and young Ole Bull would often creep in to listen, with a more than infantine curiosity, though he should at that hour have been fast asleep in bed.

At that time he was accustomed to listen, with intense interest, to the fairy-tales of his grandmother—stories about the mysterious Huldra, and the Fossekal, or Spirit of the Waterfall; and when he heard the quartetts, the child used to imagine that it was the instruments alone that sent forth all

---

[1] This magnificent picture is now the property of my mother, and hangs in the hall of her house at Putney.

those wonderful sounds. He could not conceive that the music was anything else than the singing of the violins themselves.

This was a queer notion. But Ole was a most poetic child, and a story is told of him, when he was about six years old, standing in a field before a group of blue-bells, fancying he heard them ring, and pretending to accompany their music with two pieces of wood which, in imitation of his uncle the editor, he held as a violin and bow.

After a while the worthy uncle gave little Ole a real violin, upon which the lad worked his way alone so successfully that he was soon able to take part in the quartett meetings alluded to above. His mother soon perceived this early love of music, and determined that it should be encouraged and cultivated.

At this time there was only one professor of music in Bergen, and he happened to be a violinist. His name was Poulsen; he had originally come to the old town, from Denmark, on business, but he found so many jovial companions—for Bergen has long had a reputation for conviviality—that the Danish professor postponed his departure from week to week, until he was about sixty years of age.

Poulsen, we are assured, was a true artiste; he was exquisitely sensitive to the beauties of art, had a thorough knowledge of its rules, and "would show his perseverance in playing as long as there remained a drop of brandy in the bottle set before him." When his dress was threadbare his friends would give him a new suit, and at intervals he would give a concert that would yield him a profit of about £10.

Such was the professor to whom, in his tender years, little Ole Bull was submitted for instruction. He made such rapid progress that the old professor was quite unable to do more for him, and thinking, perhaps, that his own prospects for the future were now certainly cut off in Bergen, he left the town for ever.

After that the lad took promiscuous lessons from Danish artistes, or others, who visited Bergen for a short time to give concerts. He was now twelve years old, and his father seems to have set his mind upon making him a clergyman. With that view he engaged a private tutor, who soon discovered where Ole Bull's taste lay, and forbade him to play upon his violin at all.

Placed thus under restraint, the boy's love of music became a passion; and having muffled his violin by means of a *sourdine*, or mute, he practised away at night when all was still, and nothing could be heard at Bergen save the dashing of waves upon the rocky shore and the wild strains of the lad's half-silenced violin.

So time wore on, Ole being occupied by day with his tutor and the classical authors, and at night with his dearest companion still, the little violin that his uncle had given him. He appears to have been tolerably quick in learning, and managed to satisfy his father and his tutor that he was making fair progress; so that when he had reached his eighteenth year he was despatched to Christiania to pass an examination and enter the University.

Ole Bull loved his father, and he endeavoured to follow his advice and abandon music altogether; but circumstances were too much for him. He had scarcely arrived in Christiania before he met some companions from Bergen, also students at the University, who solicited his help at a concert for the benefit of the poor. He tried to excuse himself, saying he was quite out of practice, and that his father had strictly forbidden him to play at all.

"But it is an act of charity!" they exclaimed.

"Well, that alters the case a little," replied Ole. "Perhaps my worthy parent would not mind that."

So he played at the concert.

In a little time his conscience was eased enough to join a quartett party; and when he went up, in a few days, for his examination, he was rejected.

This was his first real grief. With ill-suppressed tears, he found himself before one of the young professors at whose house he had played the night before the examination.

"It is the best thing that could have happened to you," said the latter, by way of consolation.

"How so?" inquired Ole Bull.

"My dear fellow," rejoined the other, "do you believe you are a fit man for a curacy in Finmarken or a mission among the Laps? Nature has made you a musician. Stick to your violin, and you will never regret it."

"But my father!" sobbed out the young man.

"Your father will never regret it either," said the professor.

Fortunately, his musical friends did not forsake him in these arduous circumstances. It happened that the leader of the Philharmonic Society in Christiania was very ill, and Ole Bull was appointed to fill his place *pro tem*. He managed to fulfil his duties in this capacity so well that when, some weeks later, the leader died, Bull had the position offered to him, and he accepted it.

As this rendered him independent of his father's purse, the latter, somewhat reluctantly, pardoned his failure to enter the University.

After having continued his duties as leader of the Philharmonic Society at Christiania for a whole season, and put by a little money, Bull was enabled during the vacation time in the summer of 1829, when he was not yet twenty years of age, to take a trip into Germany, where he heard Spohr (who was then director of the music at the Opera of Cassel) and several other distinguished violinists, among whom were Maurer and Wiele. He was very

OLAUS BULL

disappointed with the great Spohr. He fancied him a man who, by his personal appearance, by the poetic character of his performance, and by his genius, would enchant and overwhelm his hearers. Instead of this he found a correct teacher of exacting and cool precision in his playing, quite unable to appreciate the wild, strange melodies which Bull brought with him from the rugged, poetical land of the North.

He did not make a long stay in Germany on this occasion; and on his way home, Ole Bull fell in with some students who were going to a concert at Minden, and was induced to accompany them. It happened that the violinist of the evening was indisposed, and could not appear; it is said he had got drunk. The young Norwegian was asked to supply his place, and did so. He met with a very warm reception, and was enthusiastically applauded. Next day another warm reception attended him, on the part of the violinist who had taken too much beer on the evening of the concert. His jealousy was aroused at the success which Bull had achieved in his place, and he sent him a challenge couched in highly offensive terms.

The duel came off immediately, and Ole Bull slightly wounded his antagonist, whose hand, probably, could not have been very steady. His new friends advised him to quit the country as soon as possible, fearing this affair might lead to unpleasant consequences. So he went straight back to Christiania. There he settled quietly to work for the next year and a half; after which that restless spirit which formed an inherent part of his character induced him again to leave Norway and try his fortune in the South.

In the year 1831, when Ole Bull was scarcely one-and-twenty years of age, and whilst the cholera was raging in Paris, he found his way to that city. The diligence deposited him and his violin in the yard of the hotel. He stood there, for the first time of his life on French soil, friendless, homeless, and with an exceedingly light purse. His only resource was his violin, and his only hope that of an opportunity to make his music heard. Alas! it was a very dubious resource, and a very forlorn hope.

Crowded audiences were then attracted by the wonderful singing of the gifted Madame Malibran, and by the extraordinary performances of Paganini. All Paris was raving about these two great artistes; nothing else seemed to occupy the thoughts of the musical world. Ole Bull could not have hit upon a more inappropriate moment to pay his first visit to the French metropolis.

Of course he went to hear the two great musicians, and one night he returned very late to his lodgings, after being charmed with Malibran's singing. He flung himself on to his bed to snatch a few hours' repose, and was soon plunged in a deep sleep.

On awaking next morning, he discovered, to his utter dismay, that his landlord had absconded during the night with all his household furniture, and taking with him the musician's clothes and his violin, all of which were contained in one box of very moderate dimensions.

It is difficult to realise the dreadful situation to which poor young Ole Bull was thus suddenly reduced. He wandered about Paris for three entire days, a prey to want and despair. According to one account, he then threw himself into the river Seine, in the hope that death would relieve him from his intense anguish.

Another account says, that after being robbed of his clothes and his violin, he had still enough money in his pockets to pay for one week's accommodation in a miserable lodging-house; and it was during the last dinner for which he was able to pay that he made the acquaintance there of a well-known and very remarkable man. Ole Bull confided his miseries to this stranger, who appeared to be highly interested in his sad story. At the conclusion, after a moment's silence, the latter said abruptly—

"Well, I will do something for you, if you have courage and five francs."

"I have both," said Bull.

"Then go to-night to Frascati's at ten o'clock," continued the stranger; "pass through the first room, go into the second, where they play *rouge et noir*, and when a new *taille* begins, put your five francs on *rouge*, and leave them there."

The young musician's love of adventure, and the confidence inspired by the stranger's manner, determined him to do exactly what this peculiar individual told him. At ten o'clock precisely he stood at the celebrated gambling-house, before the table where *rouge et noir* was being played. In the course of a short time the moment came for him to act as he had been instructed. He threw his five-franc piece on *red*. The card was drawn: "Red wins," said a voice; the five francs were ten francs. The ten francs were left on *red*—in another minute they had become twenty francs. Still the young Norwegian left his money on the winning colour; and in the course of less than half an hour a considerable pile of gold lay on the table before him, and belonged to him. He had only to stretch forth his hand and gather it up.

The only question which occupied his mind was, whether he had left his money long enough? Was *red* going to pass any longer? In relating this adventure to a friend, he said, "I was in a fever; I acted as if possessed by a spirit not my own. No one can understand my feelings who has not gone through such trials—left alone in the world, as if on the extreme verge of existence, with the abyss yawning beneath, and at the same time feeling something within that should deserve a saving hand at the last moment."

Whilst he hesitated to withdraw his money, a fair white hand stretched forward towards it, and covered it. In a moment the iron grasp of the violinist had seized it by the wrist. The owner uttered a piercing shriek, and cries of "Turn her out!" were raised.

But a dark, spare figure standing near, whom Ole Bull at once recognised as his mysterious friend of a few hours previously, said in a clear, calm voice, "Madame, be good enough to withdraw your hand from that gold;" and turning to Bull, he added, "Sir, take your money, if you please."

Following this advice at once, the musician took up a sum of about four hundred francs; but he still stood riveted to the spot, and saw *red* come up to the end of the *taille;* so that had he persevered somewhat longer, he would have been a comparatively wealthy man that very evening.

He returned to his miserable lodging and counted out his gains; he could scarcely believe it was not all a dream. "What a hideous joy I felt," he says in a letter to one of his friends; "what a horrible pleasure it was to have saved one's own soul by the spoil of others!"

The strange personage who had thus befriended Ole Bull was the well-known detective, Vidocq, already an European celebrity. He never met him again.

The next thing to be done was, without waste of time, to replace the lost violin. With this object in view, he set out to purchase one; and in doing so, accidentally made the acquaintance of an individual named Lahout, who imagined he had discovered a method of imitating the old Cremona varnish by means of a compound of asafœtida which he smeared over modern-made instruments, in the hope of improving their tone. This eccentric inventor thought Bull a likely person to bring out the merits of his discovery, so he got him invited to play at a house where the Duke and Duchess de Montebello were present. His performance created a sensation, and the Duke took him at once under his patronage.

The result of this was, that Ole Bull was soon enabled to give a concert in Paris. It was not artistically so successful as it might have been; for who could listen at that time to any violinist after Paganini? However, through the kind patronage of the Duke, a large number of tickets were sold, and after paying all expenses, the young violinist found himself in possession of about 1200 francs (£48) by way of profit.

Again at this period, June 1832, a curious accident occurred to him. His landlord and landlady both died of cholera, and he was obliged to seek for new lodgings. One of his companions intimated that a lady who resided near, the Countess de Faye, had lately lost her only son, and would be glad to let his rooms for a time. He applied there, and was shown into a room where sat three ladies dressed in deep mourning. The elder one, on learning his errand, briefly declined to let him have the rooms, when one of her daughters exclaimed, "Look at him, mother!"

The violinist could not imagine what these words signified. The old lady put on her spectacles, and as she riveted her eyes upon him, her countenance suddenly changed.

She had found in Ole Bull such a resemblance to the son she had lost, that she no longer refused to let him reside in her house. Some time afterwards Ole Bull, indeed, became her son, having married the fascinating girl who had exclaimed, "Look at him, mother!"

With the little money he had now earned, he determined upon going to Italy, and provided himself with some good letters of introduction for that purpose.

He gave his first Italian concert at Milan in 1834. Applause was not wanting; but his performance was rather severely criticised in the papers. The following paragraph, reproduced from an Italian musical periodical, published shortly after this concert, probably represents very truly the state of his talent at that period :—

"M. Ole Bull plays the music of Pugnani, Spohr, Mayseder, and others, without knowing the true character of the music he plays, and partly spoils it by adding a colour of his own. It is manifest that this colour of his own proceeds from an original, poetical, and musical individuality; but of this originality he is himself unconscious. He has not yet formed himself; in fact, he has no style. Whether he is a diamond or not is uncertain, but certain it is that the diamond is not polished."

Before very long Ole Bull discovered that it was necessary to cultivate, more than he had hitherto done, his cantabile. This was his weakest point, and a most important one. In Italy he found persons who enabled him to develop this greatest quality of the violin, and from that moment his career as an artiste was more fully established.

The next concert of any consequence in which he appeared was at Bologna, and it was under rather peculiar circumstances. In fact, his reputation as a great violinist appears to date from that concert. De Bériot and Malibran were quite idolised at Bologna, and just as Ole Bull arrived in that ancient town, De Bériot was about to fulfil an engagement to play at a concert given by the celebrated Philharmonic Society. The engagement had been made by the Marquis Zampieri, a noted dilettante, who had managed to hurt the susceptibilities of the great Belgian violinist; consequently, when the day arrived, De Bériot *had a sore finger*, and, to the disappointment of all, could not play.

Ole Bull had a small lodging off one of the principal streets in Bologna, where he intended to wait until circumstances should enable him to find an audience. Meanwhile he practised assiduously at the pieces of his *répertoire*. He was thus playing in his room upstairs, his window being open, when the sound of his violin caught the ears of Madame Rossini, first wife of the celebrated composer, and once known as the charming Isabella Colbrand, *prima donna* of the San Carlo Theatre at Naples. If any one in the world could judge of the tone of a violin, she could.

Madame Rossini at once hastened to the disappointed Marquis, and informed him that she had discovered a violinist quite capable of performing in the place of M. De Bériot.

" Who is it ? " inquired the Marquis.

" I do not know," said the celebrated songstress.

" You are joking, then ? "

" Not at all; but I have assured myself that a *genius* has arrived in this town. He lodges close here," she added, pointing to Bull's apartment.

"Take your net, and catch your bird before he has flown away."

In the course of a few hours Bull was performing before a distinguished audience in the concert room of the Philharmonic Society. He played two pieces, one of which was his famous *Quartett for One Violin*. His success was considerable. The applause was most enthusiastic, and he was escorted home by a number of the members by torchlight. This was Ole Bull's first great success. He had already played in Germany, Switzerland, and in Milan, but had never created so much enthusiasm before.

Malibran was, of course, much annoyed. But so far as jealousy or anything of the kind is concerned, it never entered her amiable character nor that of De Bériot; so that shortly afterwards, when Ole Bull was introduced to them, he was received with great kindness. At this concert he also made the acquaintance of that distinguished musician, the Prince Poniatowski, and the amiable Princess, who promised him good introductions if he should go to Florence.

In 1835, in spite of the wonderful success of Paganini, he played with similar satisfactory results at Rome and Naples, and afterwards at Paris. During the ensuing year he gave concerts in other towns of France, and from the middle of 1836 to the first half of 1837 he played in London and

OLAUS BULL

the English provincial towns. In England Ole Bull gave no less than 280 concerts in sixteen months. He then made another tour, and visited almost every town of importance in Europe, and in 1843 set out for America. He returned again to Europe in 1846, continued his roving artistic life in France, Spain, Holland, &c., until 1851, the year of our first great Exhibition, when he returned to Norway, and endeavoured to establish what he termed a National Norwegian Theatre. Up to that time the Danish language only had been heard upon the Norse stage. Ole Bull desired to hear the Scandinavian language substituted for the Danish.

It was at Bergen, his native town, that he established the first Norwegian theatre, and a story is told how he got an old fiddler, named Thorgeir Andunson, a player of dance music, such as Neil Gow was in Scotland, to come and play some really national Norwegian dances in the orchestra, and thus caused the worthy old man to gain about £400 for his pains, which, of course, set him up for the rest of his days.

In 1852 Ole Bull went again to America, where he purchased some 125,000 acres of land on the banks of the Susquehanna, with the object of forming a Norwegian colony. He purchased this land from a company who had no right to sell it, as it did not belong to that company. Hundreds of Norwegian emigrants flocked there; timber was felled, ground cleared, cottages, churches, and school-houses were built, and all seemed to be progressing smoothly enough, when one morning the real owner of the property, a worthy Quaker, named George Stewardson, made his appearance on the scene. This gentleman proved to be both honest and forbearing in dealing with Ole Bull's trespass—for such it was—nevertheless, he would not consent to give up his property. Bull brought an action against the swindling company, but it nearly ruined him. He was obliged to take up his violin again to enable him to pay the law costs, whilst his opponents fought him with his own money !

Full of trouble and anxiety, he travelled from town to town, playing almost every night, until he was struck down by fever. However, his excellent constitution, which he owed greatly to his very temperate and frugal mode of living, enabled him to get over this severe attack, and with indomitable energy he at last recovered enough money to fulfil his responsibilities and realise his scheme of colonisation. He then returned to Europe, and for many years was accustomed to spend the summer on a small estate he had purchased, beautifully situated on one of the islands of the western coast of Norway, travelling south in the winter, and devoting himself to art till the very last. He died at about seventy years of age, not (as some papers announced) in 1875, but at the beginning of 1880.

OLAUS BULL

When he last visited England, in 1862, Ole Bull was a powerfully built man, with a round expressive Northern face, and thick short hair, as white as snow. He possessed a valuable Guarnerius violin. Descriptive music appears to have been his specialty. He used to say that when he played he wished to *raise a curtain* for his audience, so that they might see what was passing in his own mind, imbued with the legends and fairy-tales of the North. These he endeavoured to reproduce by the wild strains of his violin. It was a stream of melody, mixed with the harsh, discordant sounds of the surging elements. After having heard Paganini he was tempted to practise the more strange and remote difficulties of his instrument, and we have heard it said that he played the whole of the twenty-four *Capricci* of the latter from memory. We know little about his music. Besides what we have already mentioned, he had a piece called *Et Gaeterbesög*, which was intended to represent a visit to a cow-keeper's cottage on the mountain. Another was his *Battle of Kringelen*, a musical reproduction of the "Sinclair Lay" by his great-uncle.

Madame Isidora Martinez, of the Italian Opera, who sang in some concerts with him, tells me that his arpeggios were very rich, and that he had a rapid and exact staccato; also that he was perfectly at home in the concert room, and clever in ensuring a popular success.

XIII

THE CHILD VIOLINIST

IN the middle of the eighteenth century, Herr Schmöhling was a poor musician of Cassel, in Germany, where the great violinist and composer, Louis Spohr, afterwards became so well known. The little historical sketch which I am about to give opens just at the period when, yet unknown to fame, Giuseppe Guarneri was making his excellent "Del Gesu" violins, when those of Stradivari had already become famous, and when the world was hurrying on to that fatal period of revolution which has been depicted in my "Scenes from the Reign of Louis XVI."

Let the reader fix in his mind the year 1747, when there arose above the musical horizon a tiny star that shone at first with a dull, dim light, obscured by clouds of misery and misfortune, but which, when these mists were dispersed by the merciful hand of Providence, radiated glory around, illumined the Heaven of Song with a brilliancy that was dazzling, and caused beneficence to bestow its smiles where tears of sorrow were wont to flow.

THE CHILD VIOLINIST 151

The poor German artiste had never been favoured by fortune; and his suffering appears to have reached its climax when his young wife Anna, a mere girl, a charming *jungfrau*, fresh and blooming as the wild flowers of her native hills, died of fever only a few days after the birth of their first child, the subject of my narrative.

Poor before, he was now utterly miserable. The world had become a blank for him, and he cared for nothing. He became quite incapable of throwing off his despondency and emerging from the social obscurity with which he was surrounded in the dull little town.

One thing alone seemed to rouse Schmöhling's broken spirits; it was when his eyes happened to fall upon his little child, the offspring of the dearly beloved Anna, and the living image of its mother, so soon removed for ever from this world of anxious care and strife. The sight of her stimulated him to fresh exertions, though his life had lost all its charms, and misery of every kind weighed heavily upon him.

His modest and dingy lodging was on the second floor of a little house near the entrance to the town; it was of the poorest description; and now grief and distress added their mournful tints to the picture.

Whilst the father, in pursuit of daily sustenance, was absent from home—if, indeed, such a denomination can be properly applied to so miserable an abode—the poor little child was left entirely alone, attached by coarse strings to an old armchair. And as he was obliged to go out nearly every day to get his scanty living by giving a few lessons in music, or by obtaining any other musical work that offered him the chance of pocketing a few kreutzers, the little girl was left in this precarious position for many hours at a time. The effect was that she became very delicate, and at three years of age she could not walk at all. In the meantime she had been christened Elizabeth Gertrude.

As the poor father was very glad to procure any kind of work that would enable him to relieve his dire distress, he sometimes undertook to repair the instruments of the first and second violins of the Cassel orchestra. He understood pretty well the mechanism and structure of the violin, a subject on which German violinists have always prided themselves; and history reports that he was not an unskilful workman.

In those days there were not, as now, those hundreds of pianos to be tuned; nor was much to be done by selling the copyright of a song, or some small composition for stringed instruments. And repairing a violin, which in many cases only required cleaning, and a new bridge, a properly adjusted sound-post, and perhaps a little mixture of soap and chalk to make the pegs work easily, was

THE CHILD VIOLINIST 153

not to be despised as a means for paying for half a pound of cheese and a loaf or two of bread.

Then Herr Schmöhling was a violinist. Not a great one, to be sure. He could scrape, with a pupil, through the elementary exercises of his day, and see that the latter played in time and, perhaps, in tune. But in the orchestra of the little opera house, or on the trying platform of the concert room, with hundreds of eyes and ears turned upon him by people who had paid money to listen to him, he would not have cut a very brilliant figure—"it is not given to all men to go to Corinth," as the old Latin proverb said.

Sometimes, by a piece of unexpected good fortune, more than one violin at a time would be brought to his modest room to be repaired; and one day, his little daughter, then four years of age, was found playing with a violin that lay upon the table near her. After a while she took it up, and, in imitation of her father, she drew the bow across the strings, placing the tiny fingers of her left hand upon the neck of the instrument. In this way she produced, instinctively as it were, one or two notes so round and fine that Schmöhling was utterly bewildered, stopped his work, and gazed on her with his little grey eyes as wide open as nature would allow them to go.

He was lost in surprise at hearing his little girl play several notes of the scale most distinctly, before she had been taught how to do it; simply by imitating what she had seen him do. A flash of light—call it intellect, genius, instinct, or what you will—seems to have shone through the poor musician's brain at the moment. In the minutest fraction of a second he embraced every feature of the circumstance without uttering a word, like a keen-eared barrister who feels his case won by a blunder on the opposite side.

From that day forward he began systematically to teach his child music. It was a labour of love, prompted by misery and necessity, and the progress achieved under the assiduous care of a doting father was truly wonderful. In the course of some twelve months or so she could already play some little airs upon the violin, and with such a remarkable degree of skill that the precocious little girl actually became the talk of the dull old place.

It was like the spark that falls upon a haystack. Gossip spread from street to street—nothing easier to listen to in Germany than musical gossip—and every one added a little to what he or she had heard of this musical phenomenon of the old town of Cassel. It would have got into the local newspaper, but in those days this tiny sheet limited itself almost exclusively to the prices of ironstone, wood, and rye, the houses and farms that wanted tenants, a few other matters connected with the meetings of the town council, and accidents that occurred in

THE CHILD VIOLINIST 155

the streets of Berlin or some other very distant place. Paganini had not yet appeared to waken up journalists to believe in the powers of a violin; and no one had ever yet seen this instrument in the hands of a girl only five years old.

But this gossip had one curious effect—it drew around Herr Schmöhling a certain number of speculators and curiosity-mongers, several of whom made him seductive propositions with the object of exhibiting his tiny child and her violin, as they were in the habit of exhibiting giants and fat women at the fairs; for musical phenomena were rare in Cassel in those days, and, for that matter, in many other places also.

For some time the poor professor held firm to his own opinions, and refused to listen to his would-be friends, preferring to wait until his daughter's talent should be more fully developed. At last, however, he gave way, through fear of exasperating certain notabilities of the place, upon whose good graces his livelihood more or less entirely depended. And so it happened that, on the 16th of November 1753, a large room was hired for the occasion, and the little Elizabeth, then in her sixth year, made her first appearance in public. It seems almost incredible, but history has carefully recorded the whole circumstances.

The audience was numerous and select. As the poor little child could not walk, being still in very delicate health, her father carried her in his arms to the concert room. He placed her on a chair upon the platform, and put into her hands his best violin. At the first sound of the instrument a profound silence reigned throughout the room, but in a short time it was interrupted by murmurs of astonishment and approbation. At the conclusion of her first performance the applause was like thunder. The pretty little child, as she was lifted from the chair, was embraced over and over again, and large tears of joy rolled down the wizened cheeks of Herr Schmöhling as he carried his darling into the artistes' room and confided her to a circle of admiring friends. From simple curiosity the sale of tickets had been considerable, and for the first time for many years the poor musician felt that he had some money in his pocket.

What music was performed at this first concert of the child violinist it is quite impossible to say; but we may be sure that never did Orpheus with his lute, Sappho with her lyre, nor Pan with his marvellous pipes, ever produce a greater effect on the ears of mortal men or immortal nymphs. The little crippled executant, seated on the platform, went actually beyond what Paganini himself achieved many years afterwards. She produced an effect which he never did, and never could have produced, even had he lived early enough to have heard her; for, we must remember, this first concert

THE CHILD VIOLINIST 157

was in November 1753, and Paganini was born in 1784.

She charmed, she astonished, and she induced pity. It was this last effect to which I allude more particularly. Who could have been present at the concert and not experience some sentiment of this kind? Who could have seen the poor father, with privation and misery written upon his features, carrying his little child in his arms to the platform, placing her upon a chair because she was too delicate to stand, and awaiting anxiously the result of her first public performance, without feeling something more than mere curiosity? Who could have noticed the faint, nervous smile on the pretty features of the little girl, as she raised an awkward German instrument to her chin and placed the bow upon the strings, without a slight flutter of the heart, and a longing to lend a helping hand to this supreme effort, this strenuous struggle against poverty and obscurity. The loud round of applause which greeted the first performance, and brought tears into the eyes of many present, testified to all these feelings. Hearts were melted, and purse-strings were loosened, at least in one instance.

It is easy to imagine that in the little town of Cassel, for the rest of that evening, there was only one topic of conversation. But next day a most extraordinary event occurred. Herr Schmöhling received an anonymous letter containing money, and couched in the following language:—

"CASSEL, 17*th November* 1753.

"DEAR SIR,—I was one of those who experienced yesterday the greatest satisfaction on perceiving the precocious talent of your charming little daughter. It would be most regrettable that so brilliant an organisation should not receive every development of which it is susceptible. As a rich man, and a friend of art, I am decided upon defraying the expenses of her education. I beg to enclose a first instalment of 200 florins. You will proceed to Frankfort, where she will be recommended by me to the best professors, and you will receive every month a similar sum for the next ten years. In that town I have a friend, a physician of great experience, who will attend to your daughter's ailments, and I have no doubt that in a very short time she will be able to walk as well as you or I.

"I should be glad if you could start to-morrow. Do not endeavour to find out my name and address; any attempt of that sort would be displeasing and superfluous."

The letter was signed "An Amateur."

To this day I have never been able to find out who was the writer of that extraordinary letter; but, may be, it was ultimately discovered by some of those searching German historians, who appear to know everything; and one of these days it will, perhaps, be met with in the collection of some Prince or Grand Duke who devotes time to the storing up of such curiosities of artistic history. I got it from a French source, and hope it is not a pure invention.

However much, we are told, Herr Schmöhling would have liked to have wrung the hand of this magnanimous benefactor, all efforts to discover him were fruitless, and he could only abide by his instructions, which he carried out without delay.

He proceeded at once to Frankfort on the Main, where the medical skill alluded to in the letter was brought to bear with considerable success upon the little Elizabeth's affliction. The bad rearing of the infant, and indifferent nutrition, had ended by producing a paralytic condition of the legs; probably the child was rachitic. Anyhow, in the course of a few months of careful treatment, the weakness disappeared to a great extent, and at nine years of age Elizabeth Gertrude Schmöhling was as pretty a blonde German Fraulein as could have been seen anywhere in the whole kingdom. Her talent as a violinist increased as rapidly as her other charms; and wherever she played, she was the object of universal admiration.

Frankfort on the Main was a nice place in which to begin the career of an artiste. It was always gayer than Cassel, and though the latter town became, in after years, connected with the name of the eminent Louis Spohr, Frankfort was no less distinguished as the birthplace of the poet Goethe, and, many years later, it possessed, in the person of Guhr, a violinist of no mean order. In 1865, when the writer passed some time there, he was delighted with the music of the Prussian and Austrian bands, which played on alternate days at noon. Nothing ever surpassed the clarionets of the Austrian military band, and from that day to this the performances at the Opera of Frankfort have always been of the highest order.

Music had now become a very serious study with the little Elizabeth, and her mysterious benefactor, by the regularity of his remittances, enabled her father to dispense with anxiety as to the future. For five years she continued her studies and her medical treatment at Frankfort, after which it was decided to proceed to Vienna, with the view of obtaining further instruction, and, if possible, of giving some concerts. She was little more than twelve years of age when her father took her to Vienna, and arrangements were soon made for a series of concerts, in which Fraulein Schmöhling performed with great success. In a very short time she was looked upon by all the dilettanti of that gay city as the greatest musical phenomenon they had ever known. Her extreme youth, childish beauty, and elegant playing produced universal enthusiasm.

THE CHILD VIOLINIST 161

It is a curious fact, which does some honour to Great Britain, that scarcely any musical celebrity appears on the Continent but what the inhabitants of these island shores are called upon to enjoy it, and to pay for it—often to the detriment of English talent little, if at all, inferior. And yet there are (or were, not long ago) people who pretend that the English are not a musical race !

Now, it happened that among the more ardent admirers of the little German girl at Vienna was no less a personage than the English Ambassador. He actually prevailed upon her father to take her to England, and gave him several letters of introduction. The result was, that in 1760 Herr Schmöhling and his daughter set out for London, a long and tedious journey in those days. They were some months on the road, and had to undergo all those hardships of travel characteristic of the latter half of last century, of which we at the present day, with our railways, steamships, and telegraphs, can form no idea whatever. They proceeded from town to town till they reached Holland, where they gave some concerts, and at last they arrived in London, where, thanks to the letters they had brought with them, they were most kindly received.

The child was petted, as children of that age usually are, especially when they are pretty and show some remarkable artistic talent ; and many

L

are thus quite spoilt early in life. Elizabeth Schmöhling was heard at court, and in a number of concerts. Every drawing-room of any importance was graced by her presence. At the little theatre in the Haymarket she led a quartett with excellent effect. What a contrast to the life at Cassel, a few years previously! Every fop in London was raving about this wonderful German girl who played upon the violin. The attention she received from the nobility, and the universal admiration in which she was held, both for her musical talent and her graceful manners, aroused a feeling akin to jealousy in certain quarters, and it was openly asserted in many places that the violin was an *improper* instrument for a woman.

The exact significance of this condemnation I could never quite understand. All I know is, that from that time, 1760, for more than a hundred years, women who played the violin have always been very rare, until the appearance of my "Biographical Sketches of Celebrated Violinists" in 1877, when three curious events occurred. The book was brought out by the Publishers in Ordinary to Her Majesty the Queen. Shortly after its publication, Her Majesty sent to the Manchester Exhibition her picture "The Violin Player," and graciously permitted her son, the Duke of Edinburgh, to appear in public concerts as a violinist. Also, from the date of the publication of that book

THE CHILD VIOLINIST 163

to the present time the number of lady violinists has increased enormously. The cause of this coincidence must, perhaps, be sought for in the sympathy of the author for performances by ladies upon an instrument which requires so much delicacy and refinement of feeling; and no doubt this sympathy has more than once found its way into his pages.

Fraulein Schmöhling was the precursor of Theresa and Maria Milanollo, Norman Neruda, Teresina Tua, Rose Lynton, and other eminent artistes whose names nowadays would fill a whole page.

In 1760, nonsensical notions, prompted by envy and fostered by bad taste, got abroad in London to such an extent that our little German Fraulein found herself often received rather coldly, and soon became plainly convinced that the dazzling star of her fortune was not glittering so brightly as before—if, indeed, a simple maiden of thirteen could perceive such a change.

At least her father did; and it was taken into serious consideration whether it would not be best for her to abandon the violin and cultivate her voice, which was naturally powerful, sweet, and flexible. It would only require a little training to enable her to rival the greatest singers of the day.

Curious to relate, this voice is said to have extended from G to E, more than two and a half octaves, the exact compass of the violin as generally used in those days.

In the last half of the eighteenth century there lived in London an Italian named Paradisi, who had earned a considerable reputation as a professor of singing, though still quite a young man. Schmöhling determined to place his daughter under his tuition, and Paradisi soon discovered that he had on his hands a pupil of no ordinary talent. Not only was her voice of great extent and extreme flexibility, but she possessed exquisite feeling and marvellous dramatic instinct. In a very short time her advancement in this new capacity was so notable, that she actually appeared at some public concerts in London, and obtained a very considerable success.

Some say that this success excited a great amount of jealousy; and others, perhaps with greater truth, assert that Paradisi proposed to *farm*—as well as to form—the talent of the young songstress for a certain number of years, a proposition to which Herr Schmöhling would not agree. Hence there arose a quarrel between them; and the result was that no more engagements were forthcoming, but only invidious comments and calumnies; so that the poor father and daughter were soon reduced to the greatest straits.

Poverty again stared them in the face!

Having scraped together, by whatever means

THE CHILD VIOLINIST 165

they could, enough coin to enable them to reach their native country, they set out for Cassel, where it was hoped to obtain some kind of an engagement. But here again the poor man was deceived. There was no opening whatever for his talented daughter.

By this time, however, the girl had begun to think for herself. Her ambition and her perseverance knew no bounds. She had heard of a famous man named Hiller. He had founded a music school at Leipzig in 1766, and it had already gained some notoriety. Elizabeth Gertrude Schmöhling studied there until the year 1771, when she was twenty-two years of age. Her voice was at that period one of the finest ever heard, and, with the sole exception of Henrietta Sontag, she was probably the greatest singer that Germany has ever produced.

To follow her career in these pages as a *prima donna* would be out of place. After having made her *début* at Dresden, and sung in various other opera houses, where she shone principally in the music of Jomelli, Porpora, Sacchini, Hasse, Picini, and Glück, she ended by enchanting that eminent amateur flautist, Frederick the Great, at Berlin—a man who until then had never much believed in German music. She was appointed court musician at a salary of 3000 florins, which did not much interfere with her theatrical career.

It was at Potsdam, during these Berlin engagements, that the 'cello player, Giovanni Mara, who was in the Royal Orchestra, made love to her and married her; and it is as Madame Mara that her name has come down to posterity as one of the greatest singers of that or any other period.

The marriage was not a happy one, and added to the many troubles and vicissitudes of the artiste's life. To relate these alone would occupy a whole volume. After appearing with great success in Vienna and Paris, Madame Mara came again to London—no longer as a child violinist, but as the most celebrated *prima donna* in the whole of Europe. Her style was serious, rather than of the *buffa* character, and in London her singing at the Handel Festivals was the subject of conversation for a lengthened period.

In London she appeared with the celebrated Mrs. Billington (another lady of German extraction) and the great Italian cantatrice, Brigitta Banti. At her farewell appearance in 1801, when she was fifty-five years of age, the receipts were over a thousand pounds sterling—a very great sum in those days. From 1806 to 1813 Madame Mara resided at Moscow, and when that town was burnt she lost considerable property which she had purchased there. She then retired to Revel, where she supported herself by giving lessons in music, and where she died in January 1833. On the celebra-

THE CHILD VIOLINIST 167

tion of her eighty-third birthday, in 1831, the poet Goethe addressed some verses to her.

To properly appreciate such a woman as Mara, her life should be read in all its minutest details; but these are only to be found scattered through numerous publications, and no complete biography of this most wonderful singer exists. I have only dwelt here on her career as a youthful violinist, and her early struggles to rise from poverty and neglect to the very highest position in the musical world. It was her upright character and generosity, as much as her extraordinary talent, that enabled her to soar above the hypocrisies, jealousies, and calumnies of that rakish age; and her career, like that of Banti, Sontag, and some other great singers whom we could name, was one of a highly romantic and dramatic character.

What became of her violin? Did she preserve it, as Madame Nilsson has preserved hers? Was it burnt in the dreadful fire at Moscow? What interest that violin would arouse if it were still to be found, and could be duly authenticated!

Alas! it is rare indeed that any violin can be authenticated; and no one who knows anything of the life of Madame Mara, her wonderful career at the Operas of Berlin, Vienna, Paris, London, and the vicissitudes of such an active life, the energy of which was kept up to the very last, would be likely to credit any trumped-up pedigree of an old instrument put forward for lucrative purposes.

It is said that the violin of Corelli is still to be seen; a double-bass said to have belonged to the famous Dragonetti was exhibited some few years ago in London; and Paganini's violin—unless it has been changed—still stands in the Museum at Genoa, with that of Camillo Sivori, now by its side.

An English gentleman, an amateur violinist travelling in Germany, where he paid a visit to the great poet Goethe at the beginning of this century, brought back with him from Weimar a yellow German violin, said to be the instrument that had originally belonged to Fraulein Schmöhling, then known as the eminent *prima donna*, Madame Mara. This instrument is now in the possession of a member of that gentleman's family; it has a very fine tone, and is prized as one of the greatest of curiosities.

In recent years, Madame Nilsson, Madame Sembrich, Mademoiselle Singeli (Singelée), and several others whom I could name, are examples of eminent singers who have abandoned the violin for the voice. The former has, however, one great advantage—it lasts longer than the most robust vocal organs; and we have in Tartini, Nardini, Sainton, and several others, instances of violinists who have performed admirably when over seventy years of age. Madame Mara used to say that had she a

THE CHILD VIOLINIST

daughter to whom singing was to be taught, this daughter should first study the violin; and she attributed in great measure to her violin training that wonderful facility in vocal execution which astonished and charmed her audiences in every city of Europe.

XIV

THE ORCHESTRA AND THE SINGER

IN our days, when almost every orchestral player is a thorough artiste, having been obliged to follow out a long and arduous course of study, and has, in too many cases, to eke out his moderate income by giving music lessons, it may be useful to say a few words about the remuneration which these excellent musicians receive.

Some years ago, in my "Biographical Sketches of Celebrated Violinists," I asked the important question: Why do we make so great a distinction between the remuneration of singers and that of instrumentalists? Why do we pay a *prima donna* or a *primo tenore*—often of rather limited musical education—by some hundreds of guineas a night, when the leading violin—often a highly educated musician — is obliged to content himself with a guinea, or under special circumstances, say, two guineas? It seems perfectly monstrous!

These questions apply, of course, to the orchestras of the opera and the concert room. When any of the members of such an orchestra happens

THE ORCHESTRA AND THE SINGER 171

to perform a solo, we perceive at once of what first-rate artistes it is composed; but we can perceive it still more by listening attentively to their joint performance.

The enormous sums paid to the leading singers, together with the high rent of the building, form the chief causes of the comparatively low salaries of instrumentalists, and of the price of seats at the opera being quite beyond the reach of many thousands of the public. These persons, in England, are obliged to be content with the strains and antics of the music hall, though they would enjoy the opera much more, and become useful patrons of music were they not thus excluded.

If things were otherwise, instead of having one or perhaps two opera houses in the hands of *quasi* millionaires, we should have, may be, a dozen in the London district alone, managed on a more moderate scale and better principles. This would also promote the interests of composers, of whom we possess not a few of very considerable abilities, who have now scarcely a chance of being heard. The time cannot be far distant when this most unsatisfactory state of things will be rectified.

As regards violinists, it is true that, now and then, a modern Paganini will arise and take a glorious revenge; but that is not exactly the point in question. Without an orchestra there can be no opera, no oratorio; and if we wish to keep up our lyric stage to a high pitch of perfection, we must give our musicians, especially the orchestra and the chorus, proper encouragement, and something to look forward to.

I remember hearing a certain octet in Rossini's opera, *Matilda di Sabran*, which is considered very fine; but it struck me at the time that it would have been still finer with an orchestral accompaniment, however slight, from the pen of the same great master.

That the actual state of things urgently needs reform is the more evident when we consider that it is not every violinist, or flautist, who can shine forth as a solo-player, and go on his travels rejoicing—though some of my friends spend almost all the money they earn on the concert platform in luxurious hotel expenses, &c., and it is certainly a sad thing when a man returns from tour to his hard-working wife, who has been giving laborious lessons all the time, with nothing but a cigar in his pocket!

It is not every orchestral musician, however clever, that can derive great benefits by travelling as a solo-player. The education is different after a certain stage of perfection has been attained; and the qualities admired in the one are different from those we applaud in the other: the orchestral player is trained to sacrifice himself for the *ensemble*, whilst the solo-player is educated to bring forth all

THE ORCHESTRA AND THE SINGER 173

his *individuality* or originality. Hence two classes of musicians, who can rarely take each other's place.

When we compare the salaries of the singers with those of our first-rate orchestral artistes, it becomes evident that the latter are as much undervalued as the soprani, tenori, and bassi are overvalued.

How is this state of things to be remedied ?

The problem is as simple as the first proposition of Euclid; all we have to do is to reduce the exorbitant salaries to a reasonable figure, and raise the others.

Some clever men may, perhaps, exclaim that this is much "easier said than done." But that remark applies to most things in life, and, as De Bériot once said about violin playing, an artiste is never quite willing to do all he can do.

What I contend for is reasonable salaries all round, cheaper places, and a greater number of opera houses.

Is not a leading violin, 'cello, or flute on a par in every respect with a leading singer ? Is not his education as good, or better, and his performance as praiseworthy and valuable ? Why, then, this enormous gap between the salaries of the two ?

Of course, we know why. It is the encouragement of what is called the "star" system, and what we must endeavour to find out is the most effectual manner of putting a stop to it.

The above remarks are more especially applicable to English players of stringed instruments. The grievance I complain of affects them far more than their fellow-musicians in Italy, Germany, and France. Almost all our best violinists are men of the orchestra. Two centuries ago John Bannister told Charles II. that the English violinists were superior to those of France—it is a pity he did not compare them also to the foreign singers of his day—but however that may be, it is high time that there should exist a more equal distribution of salary between the opera singer and the members of the orchestra.

XV

SECRETS OF THE "CREMONA VIOLIN" TRADE

AN immense amount of money, probably over a million sterling, is annually circulated in buying and selling "Cremona" violins. Dealers in what has been justly called the king of instruments are dispersed all over the country, as well as in the large towns. Their agents crop up when least expected, even in small, unheard-of villages.

Suppose a gentleman who is not a musician wishes to dispose of a valuable old instrument that has come to him as an heirloom or otherwise, and that he inserts an advertisement to that effect in some musical paper. In reply to this advertisement he receives a certain number of letters, chiefly from dealers, or rather their agents, often from country agents of London dealers. He is requested to *name his price* (or, perhaps, a very low offer is made), and he is invited to forward the instrument for approval, by rail or carrier, duly *insured* against loss or injury.

If he is wise, he replies that he will do so on receipt of a cheque for the value he puts on the violin, which money will be refunded if the instrument should not be approved of, and is returned to him uninjured in the course of a month. This proposition, aided by good references, is at once accepted. The cheque having been duly honoured, the violin is forwarded as directed. In the course of a week or so it is returned, with a letter to the effect that "So-and-so" of London pronounces it not to be a genuine Cremona; the amount of the cheque is requested to be refunded at once, and *a low price is offered for the violin at the same time.*

The instrument is none the better for its journey; probably the box is split or scratched, and the violin itself slightly injured, but not seriously enough to enable the owner to claim much damages.

On the other hand, if the advertisement is perchance answered by a private individual, he refuses to buy unless the instrument is guaranteed genuine by a regular dealer; and it is a well-known fact that no dealer will guarantee any violin to be genuine in which he is not personally interested.

Such being the case, there is only one way to get the true value of an old Cremona violin, namely, to place it (with a reserved price) in a public auction. That was the plan adopted by Charles Reade, the writer, who had some experience in these matters, and occasionally dealt in valuable instruments. It is the only means, except on rare occasions, by which a private person, however good a judge of violins he may happen to be, will find himself a match for the dealers in Cremona instruments.

There has existed for the last fifty years or more a craze—I can call it by no other name—for old "Cremona" violins. Now, in the whole world there are really (as Rossini said for music) *only two kinds of violins*—those which are good, and those which are bad. Almost every violin of superior tone and of great age is dubbed a "Cremona," and duly labelled with an imitation-old label. From the beginning of the sixteenth century to the end of the eighteenth there have been many other makers besides those of Cremona who have turned out violins quite equal to the latter, and even more modern makers have done as much.

Among the former I should mention Sebastian Kloz, of Mittenwald, in the Tyrol; Scheinlein, of Stuttgard (recommended by the great Spohr); Simon, of Salzburg (the birthplace of Mozart, though his violin was by Maier, of the same town), and several others. So that it is really absurd to attach such exclusive importance to the old city of Cremona. It is a craze, as I said before, which is kept up as much as possible for trade purposes. As a proof of this, I myself have had in my hands violins by Sebastian Kloz, Hünger, Simon, Lupot, and others, which were quite equal to, if not better than, Amati, Stradivari, and Guarneri violins with which I have had the opportunity of comparing them.

Only a short time ago I heard a violoncello, by quite a modern maker, which gave a finer tone than a similar instrument by Ruggeri, of Cremona, heard at the same time; and I remember reading of a trial of instruments before an Academical Commission at Paris, the violins being played by the then famous Boucher, when an instrument by Chanot was unanimously declared finer than one by Stradivarius with which it was compared.

To the general public, violins and 'cellos of the same pattern and of a certain age, made by different makers and in different countries, are exceedingly difficult to distinguish one from the other. There is the flat model of Stradivarius, Sebastian Kloz, Hünger, Lupot, &c., and the raised pattern of Amati, Ruggeri, Mathias Kloz, Stainer, Albani, &c. English makers, such as Barnes, Forster, Duke, Perry, Fendt, and others, have followed both these models, and it is often quite impossible to distinguish their instruments from violins of foreign origin.

An immense amount of error has been diffused with regard to varnish. The "amber" colour of many Stradivarius violins has been translated into amber (*succinum*) used in the varnish! And the term "grand" Amati has been taken to mean violins of a *grand quality*, whereas it was only meant

THE "CREMONA VIOLIN" TRADE 179

to indicate *size*, these instruments being a rather *larger model* than the small-pattern violins that were usually made by the Amatis and Guarneris, Guadagninis, and others.

It has been said, over and over again, that the old Cremona varnish is a lost art. This is mere nonsense. We have only to look into the technical works of the seventeenth and eighteenth centuries to see how the varnish was made and coloured. The old Cremona makers are supposed to have used "oil-varnish," like our coachbuilders; but the varnish on a Stradivarius is attacked and dissolved by spirit, which shows it is not an oil-varnish. When prejudice, fostered by trade interests, is put aside, the Cremona craze will disappear entirely. Dealers keep it up, of course, and every superior violin, whoever may have made it, is called a "Cremona," and an imitation-old label stuck into it. With regard to labels, here is an experiment which is instructive.

A good orchestral violin of modern make had the label of the maker in it when purchased. After twenty-four years' constant work in the orchestra and out of it, this label had become perfectly invisible; it was covered with black dust and rosin, and no amount of rubbing with grease, spirit, soap and water, &c., would restore it. During this treatment it was destroyed. If this be the effect of only twenty-four years' use, what are we to say of those easily-read labels purporting to have been over two hundred years in a violin?

It is known that several old makers like Stainer, for instance, did not use printed labels, but wrote them; others, like Sebastian Kloz, impressed the initials of their names on some spot in the inside or outside of the violin.

A curious thing happened to a friend of mine in 1893 and 1894. In the spring of the first-named year, he took an old Italian violin to a West End dealer for disposal, and I went with him. He expected the latter to make him an offer for it, but the dealer insisted on *the owner naming his own price.* At last he did so, and asked £70 for an instrument well worth more than double that amount. The dealer then said the instrument was not what it was supposed to be, and though the tone was very fine, he *could not possibly sell it without a name.* Next year the same gentleman took another valuable violin to the same dealer, who told him this time that the tone was not so good as it might be, and that the *name of the maker was of no account, tone alone being what was now required* in the violin market. That was certainly a most singular change of opinion in the short period of twelve months!

Age mellows a violin, especially if it has been constantly in use; it renders the tone softer and the stroke of the bow smoother, but *it will never alter the quality of the tone,* as this depends upon the *form* of the instrument, and its *thickness in various places.* Some old Amati and Guarneri violins are certainly rather nasal, a fault which can never be remedied. A nasal-toned instrument will always remain nasal. A harsh violin will become less harsh by long use; but when harsh, and nasal, and loud, nothing will ever improve it.

It is not difficult to find loud violins; the difficulty is to find those which are sufficiently powerful, but rich and sweet at the same time. Violins of a flat model are generally louder, and carry farther than those of a raised model; the latter are sometimes sweeter in tone, but often very nasal, reminding us of the sound of a hurdy-gurdy. An instrument of this description is unpleasant even to uneducated ears. When the sound-post is in the proper place, well cut, and perfectly perpendicular, and the bridge exactly suits the instrument as regards thickness, height, and quality of wood, the tone should be smooth and equal, sweet, and sufficiently powerful, without any nasal quality whatever. No difference of tone should be perceptible when the bow passes from one string to another (this is termed "equality"), and the note should be easily caused to swell under increased pressure of the bow—this quality gives "brilliancy."

Modern players who possess instruments of no great name generally dislike to have it thought that they are playing on a "Cremona" of great value; and if you happen to compliment them on their fine tone, they at once take care to make known that their instrument is *a very ordinary one, by no great maker.*

I have before referred to the fact mentioned by Dancla that he preferred his own violin, which was made by Gand of Paris, to a fine Stradivari instrument, the loan of which was offered to him for one of his concerts.

In spite of all that has been said on this subject, there is little doubt possible that, in the course of their work, the Cremona makers, especially Nicolo Amati, Antonio Stradivari, Ruggeri, Giuseppe Guarneri, Lorenzo Guadagnini, turned out some violins and basses of the very finest description imaginable. And such an instrument to a player is simply invaluable. The violins of these makers, like those of Sebastian Kloz and Stainer, are extremely rare, and are becoming more so every day.[1] Stradivari made the greatest number of any (but they were not all

---

[1] In his series of articles on Cremona instruments, published in 1872, on the occasion of the Loan Exhibition in London, Charles Reade speaks of a Stradivarius violin which belonged to Vuillaume. He says, "This Vuillaume-Stradivarius is worth, as times go, £600 at least." The instrument in question was recently bought for £2000 by Mr. Crawford, a Yorkshire gentleman, from the executors of Alard, the celebrated professor of the violin at the Paris Conservatoire, and son-in-law of Vuillaume. It is supposed to be *just as it was turned out by the great Cremona maker*, having been very little played on, and never opened. It has thus more than trebled in price in twenty years.

equally good), and his violins have been more copied than any others; so that his celebrated name is likely to be kept green for many centuries to come, though several makers in the Tyrol have more than once equalled, if not surpassed him.

XVI

THE VIOLIN SCHOOL AT NEUILLY

COMING from the second floor of a plain, solidly built, commodious house at Neuilly, just outside Paris, might be heard, many years ago, the sweet tones of a fine Amati violin which, during the summer months, when the windows were open, would attract the attention of passers in the street below, more than one of whom tarried a while to listen to a delicious piece of melody, or a closing cadenza of surprising elegance.

There lived in this house a celebrated violinist —whom, for motives of convenience, we shall call Lanfredi — who, after having astonished and charmed for more than a quarter of a century the whole musical world of Europe, had finally settled down as a teacher, bent upon devoting the remainder of his life to initiating a few chosen pupils into the secrets of his marvellous talent.

In order that his name and his method might with more certainty go down to posterity, he was careful in the choice of his pupils. He only took young men who gave some decided proof of pos-

THE VIOLIN SCHOOL AT NEUILLY 185

sessing a natural gift for music; youths who had already gone through the preliminary solfeggio and elementary studies, and on whom his time would not be expended in vain. He desired to leave behind him a name and a school, as Tartini and Viotti had done—singular craving, which is inherent in all human nature.

"What is fame!" scornfully exclaimed the gifted Lord Byron; yet no man ever strived harder for it than he did. What is it that induces men and women to wish to become famous, and to be talked of hereafter as honoured specimens of their race? As we cannot realise the ravings of the old alchemists and become physically immortal, the next thing is to strive for a moral immortality—but, is it not a craze like the other? Anyhow, it is an essential part of human nature, and should not be despised; for it tends to the leading of exemplary lives, and is sometimes well rewarded on this side of the tomb.

Lanfredi had led an exemplary life. He was a robust and an ambitious man, sixty-five years of age, and a bachelor, a man of simple tastes and generous disposition. His violin playing had shed a halo of glory around his name, and now that he had retired with a moderate competency from the platform of the concert room, he was desirous of prolonging his brilliant reputation.

Being so particular in the choice of his pupils, it

may be easily imagined that Lanfredi's music class mustered, at most, about a dozen violinists, young and ardent musicians of considerable promise. Among them there were two youths of about the same age, but of very opposite characters and appearance. Both were clever instrumentalists, who only required a year or two of finishing lessons to improve their style, and to see them develop into *virtuosi* of the very first rank.

One was a tall, fair, well-proportioned youth, just twenty years of age, named Gustave Lafont; and the other, Maurice Stein, an Alsatian, was rather under medium height, and of a dark complexion. In spite of their different dispositions they were excellent friends, brothers in art, enthusiastic in the promotion of each other's welfare—united, in fact, by bonds of the warmest affection.

They were both handsome young men in their respective styles of beauty. Gustave was, perhaps, the most gifted by nature in this respect, having a frank, open countenance, large blue eyes, and a modest, sensitive demeanour, which was certainly attractive. His friend Maurice had a somewhat impetuous disposition, his temper was easily ruffled, but he was naturally generous and enthusiastic.

These were the two favourite pupils of Lanfredi, and he foresaw for both of them a brilliant artistic career. In music they ranked very much on a par.

THE VIOLIN SCHOOL AT NEUILLY 187

Gustave's playing was the more elegant and expressive, but that of Maurice was in the highest degree brilliant. The old professor often turned to these young artistes, and pointed them out to his friends as the coming stars of the violin firmament, which would shine with the brightest light. He looked upon them almost as if they were his own children, and there was nothing he would not do to contribute to their welfare and to secure the advancement of their ambitious desires. Already, indeed, had he done much in this respect.

The two young violinists were in rather different circumstances. Gustave Lafont was a penniless orphan. His father, with several other Frenchmen, was killed in the streets during an insurrection at Valparaiso, and his mother died shortly after arriving in France, having fled to her native country to escape the horrors of revolution in a small South American republic. She left but little money, and Gustave, who was then barely fifteen years of age, inherited a sum which may be represented by about £300, as the total residue of his mother's estate. Law expenses, travelling expenses, and the low price realised by her little property sold in Chili accounted for all the rest.

Before the whole of this little sum was spent he had been placed in the Paris Conservatoire through the intervention of a kind lawyer, one of the executors, on whom had devolved the unremunerative task of winding up the affairs; and he was still studying music there when accident thrust him in the way of the veteran violinist Lanfredi. The latter took kindly to the poor boy, assisted him in many ways, and finally allowed him to live in a little room at the top of his own house, and to partake of his meals at the professor's frugal board. In return for this, Gustave helped Lanfredi by copying music, by repeating with some of the younger pupils the daily scale exercises, and in making himself generally useful to the old musician. He was more like a devoted son to him than anything else.

Such had been the state of things for more than a year when Maurice Stein joined the violin class, and as his musical talent was already very remarkable, the two youths soon became very great friends. It was an exceedingly agreeable acquaintance for Gustave, and a highly distinguished pupil for Lanfredi.

Maurice Stein lived in the neighbourhood with his mother, a widow whose late husband, a silk mercer, had left her a small fortune equivalent to about £120 a year English money, and the son possessed (or would possess at the age of twenty-five) from his grandfather's will about £80 a year, which his mother also enjoyed, allowing him amply sufficient to provide for his modest expenses at the café or the billiard-room. He would not come of

THE VIOLIN SCHOOL AT NEUILLY 189

age, according to French law, till he was twenty-five, and as yet his years numbered but one-and-twenty. He had loved his violin since he was a mere child, and it had been decided by all the members of his family that he should adopt the musical profession, as he showed extraordinary capacities in this respect. His grandfather, who had been a distinguished performer on the spinet, had given him, when almost a baby, a fine Gasparo da Salo violin possessing a powerful and sweet tone, which the lad soon knew how to produce to the best advantage.

The terrorist days of the French Revolution had passed; Napoleon Buonaparte had played his wonderful *rôle* in the history of modern Europe; Cherubini had left his position as head of the Paris Conservatoire for a better world; and the French people, after having executed their good-natured king, Louis XVI., when he was only thirty-eight years of age, had seen his brother, Louis XVIII., reign over them for many years, and had then placed his other brother, Charles X., upon the throne, awaiting the momentous crisis of 1830, which no one appears to have foreseen.

Paris had, in fact, settled down into a quiet, humdrum life, exhausted as it was by the horrors and excitement of previous years. The musical war of the Glückists and Piccinists had been fought out long ago, and had been succeeded by that of the Maratists and Todists, in which Madame Mara, the "child violinist," or rather her adherents, had gained the day. In 1829 Rossini brought out his immortal *Guillaume Tell*, which helped, no doubt, the revolution of the following year, when Charles X. fled to Scotland, and became accustomed to the music of the bagpipes.

In 1831 Paganini paid his first visit to Paris, and astonished every one, exhibiting the utmost powers of the violin, and producing the most extraordinary effects at all his concerts.

Lanfredi was an admirer of the sublime Viotti, and continued his excellent style and method in spite of the startling innovations of the great Genoese violinist. In the hands of his pupil, Gustave Lafont, the broad style of Viotti breathed forth anew in the most superb melodies, whilst the impetuous nature of Maurice Stein tended more in the direction of the brilliant school of Paganini, but, under the superior instruction of his distinguished master, he blended the two together, after the manner of De Bériot.

Maurice was a spoilt child. His mother gave way too readily to all his whims and caprices. He was passionately fond of music, and the forced study to which he subjected himself, in order to satisfy his craving for celebrity, had acted upon his nerves, rendering him irritable, morose, passionate, and at times even violent. In this respect he formed a marked contrast to his friend Gustave,

THE VIOLIN SCHOOL AT NEUILLY 191

whose quiet, good-humoured nature, though full of animation, was rarely much ruffled by untoward events.

The respective characters of these young violinists developed themselves not only in their music, but in every little detail of their lives. Nothing akin to jealousy was ever evoked between them. It would have been perfectly absurd to say that either of them was superior to the other. Both would be unanimously awarded the warmest applause; both would be admitted to have attained the highest excellence. Not unfrequently, during their student life, Gustave and Maurice would join in playing some duet which had been composed by their talented master, when each one threw into it the charm of his particular style, to the great delight of all those who were privileged to hear such a fine performance.

Musical evenings, to which a few intimate friends were invited, occasionally enlivened the life of the old professor and his pupils. On one of these evenings Gustave and Maurice performed a duet with piano accompaniment upon a touching melody from Rossini's *Gazza Ladra*. This created such an impression upon the audience, mostly composed of good musicians, that the violinists were obliged to repeat it. At the conclusion of the piece tears of joy could be seen streaming down the cheeks of the worthy old Lanfredi, whilst the two young artistes clasped themselves in each other's arms, amidst the enthusiastic applause of the guests. From that moment Gustave and Maurice vowed a lifelong friendship.

Four years were thus passed—four most enjoyable years—by the end of which time these pupils of Lanfredi had become two of the finest violinists in the capital. During the whole of that time nothing had ever occurred to slacken in any degree the ties of affection which bound them together. However, a period arrived when a great change took place, under circumstances over which the young musicians had no control whatever, which not only broke into their deep feelings of mutual friendship and admiration, but influenced the ultimate course of their hitherto tranquil existence, and that of Lanfredi himself.

· · · · ·

Lanfredi was a bachelor, as we have already intimated, but we do not believe in bachelors. Doubtless more than one romantic episode could be put to his account, for he was a man of a poetic and sensitive nature. Like Tartini of old, his parents had destined him for the Church or the Bar, but his love of art took him away from these professions, and he drifted into that of music. Born near Lecco, on a branch of the Lago di Como, he made his first public appearance at Milan, where he had been educated. His success on that occasion was so remarkable, that he had ever since led a wandering artistic life, full of engagements, and after a long and successful career he had finally settled as a violin teacher at Neuilly, as we have seen. Being a man of great and varied resources, equally fond of history, literature, and musical composition, he depended little for amusement on the outside world. His position as an artiste, combined with a good stock of general information and experience, fitted him for the best society in the French capital. But his simple tastes and moderate means kept him much at home. His greatest pleasure was to listen to the conversation of a few intimate friends, or to the performance of some really excellent music at those little social gatherings to which we have alluded. Why he did not mix more in the aristocratic circles, to which he received frequent invitations, is not very difficult to understand. Many grand personages asked him chiefly with the idea that he would charm the company by his playing, and he was often bored by allusions to sports and entertainments, political speculations, and commercial enterprises, in which neither his tastes nor his modest fortune permitted him to take the slightest interest. A quiet cigar and a little gossip over a cup of coffee in the company of one or two sympathetic friends was far more acceptable to him than the most crowded room of the most *élite* society that Paris could offer. Nevertheless, when he did happen to appear with his violin, he had the whole room at his feet.

With all this Lanfredi was a large-hearted, generous man, and scarcely a day passed that some poor person had not cause to bless his liberality. His domestic affairs were managed by an active and intelligent housekeeper named Ninette, who appeared to be always busy, and a stout girl of sixteen who was not remarkable for activity.

For many long years he had lived with the sole society of his violin. He was now contented with his past life and his present position. If asked why he never married, he would reply facetiously that he looked upon man as a being incapable of serving two mistresses at the same time, and he was wedded to art.

Among the severest trials of his middle age had been the sudden death of a younger brother, who left alone in the world a little girl barely twelve years of age. This orphan child Lanfredi had brought from Italy and adopted as his own daughter. She was placed at a large boarding-school in Paris, where every comfort and a good education were provided for her. But the time had now arrived when she was old enough to be received into her uncle's house, and to take the management of it upon herself. About this time, also, an engagement in the orchestra at the Opera had been obtained for Gustave.

THE VIOLIN SCHOOL AT NEUILLY 195

Paulina Lanfredi was then eighteen years of age, a beautiful and accomplished brunette, one of the most charming young persons that ever graced a Parisian home. Her dark expressive eyes, bewitching smile, elegant figure, and amiable disposition were sure to attract universal attention. The old professor, who was quite proud of her, could not help feeling that the management of his household would, probably, soon again devolve upon his faithful old housekeeper; for Paulina, with all her domestic tastes, her innocence of the ways of the world, and her love of music, which was only surpassed by her devotion to her uncle, would soon have numerous admirers, and it would be impossible to keep such a beautiful bird in his lonely cage for any length of time.

The return home of Paulina was the occasion of great festivity at the violin school. All Lanfredi's best friends were invited to take part in it. A dinner party and concert were to celebrate this auspicious event; and covers were laid for twenty guests. The day was delicious—it was the 10th of June 1831—and Lanfredi's smiling features beamed with delight and animation.

Paulina had arrived early in the morning a few days previously, and was already installed in her newly prepared apartments. She was now busy with Ninette preparing for the evening's amusement. The two violinists, Gustave and Maurice, were present when she arrived. They had both seen her before, on those rare occasions when, during the vacations, she spent a few weeks at her uncle's house. But now they were both very much impressed by her appearance. She was no longer the insignificant little school-girl of a few years ago, but quite a young lady—and a very handsome young lady.

All the violin pupils had been invited to the dinner, and some of Lanfredi's oldest friends. The composer Rossini was to be among the audience at the concert, and Madame Pasta had promised to sing. She was then on her way to London from Milan, where she had just created a great impression by her singing in the first performance of Bellini's *Sonnambula*, and was a great friend of the veteran violinist. Lanfredi's niece, who was already a clever pianist, was to perform a solo, and to accompany Gustave and Maurice in their violin pieces.

We shall not attempt to describe the dinner. All the guests arrived punctually, some of the pupils bringing their sisters, so that there were several pretty faces in the room. Rossini and Madame Pasta arrived after dinner, and joined the party in the little garden, where Ninette had provided coffee, under an awning that sheltered the guests from the heat of the afternoon sun. Every one seemed delighted, and our two violinists even more so than any one else.

Neither the curious stories of Lanfredi's adventures in Russia, nor the witty anecdotes told by Rossini, which kept the company in roars of laughter, could prevent Gustave and Maurice from keeping their eyes fixed on Paulina. They had little opportunity of speaking to her, and when such an opportunity did occur, they both wanted to speak together. The dark eyes and brilliant laughter of Lanfredi's niece had captivated every one present, but especially the two young violinists. For the first time in his life Gustave seemed rather vexed with Maurice—it was when he paid any little attention to Paulina; and, on his side, Maurice was decidedly ruffled when he observed that Gustave seemed so much pleased at addressing a few words to her alone.

The sun had scarcely sunk below the horizon when Lanfredi summoned his guests into the music room, and the concert began. It commenced by a fantastic quartett, very well played by the younger pupils; and then Paulina gave a piano solo by Panseron, which was much applauded, and was the occasion of endless compliments, in which Gustave and Maurice, of course, had their share. Madame Pasta then most good-naturedly sang a lovely *aria* which had just been written for her by the young composer Bellini, after which Rossini seated himself at the piano and sang his own *Largo al Factotum*, which created an immense impression. It was now the turn of Maurice to play a violin solo, and Paulina accompanied him. It was a strange, weird composition, which he appeared to have chosen especially for her. The execution was in the highest degree remarkable, and the applause vociferous, but the heart of the young maiden evidently remained unmoved.

Not so, however, when after several more beautiful pieces had been heard, including the violin duet on the lovely motive from the *Gazza Ladra* —not so when Gustave played, in his turn, a violin solo to the accompaniment of Paulina. This time the instrument told a tale of love and hope that could not be misunderstood. It pleased the audience exceedingly, but it seemed to touch the charming niece of Lanfredi still more. Maurice perceived this at once. A feeling of savage rivalry was awakened in his breast. The piece had no sooner concluded than, taking up his violin case, he left the house without a word of adieu to any one; and Gustave, to his utter astonishment, found that his friend had gone without that cordial shake of the hand to which he had been so long accustomed. He did not realise the motive of this sudden departure, and feared that Maurice was ill. He was ill; but it was a malady that affects many young men, and with which, according to Shakespeare, no medical art can grapple.

• • • • • •

THE VIOLIN SCHOOL AT NEUILLY 199

For a long time past Lanfredi had been accustomed to stroll out after dinner, and to enjoy his cigar at a café about a mile from the house. But since his niece had returned he had given up this habit, and preferred to take coffee with her. Sometimes on a Sunday afternoon, when they went out, Gustave would accompany them in their walk; but he otherwise saw little of Paulina, for by this time he was regularly employed at the Opera. Nevertheless, an affectionate friendship had sprung up between them, and seemed not likely to diminish as time advanced.

One Sunday evening, indeed, an opportunity occurred which gave the young violinist a chance of declaring to Paulina the admiration which he felt for her and could no longer conceal. It was raining; they had not gone out with the veteran professor that afternoon, and Lanfredi, who had enjoyed a good dinner, had just fallen asleep in his arm-chair. The two young people had carried on a conversation in a low tone of voice, when suddenly Paulina exclaimed—

"Oh, what an avowal, Monsieur Gustave!"

"You refuse me?" asked Gustave excitedly.

"But who could have dreamt of it?" said Paulina. "You really frighten me!"

"You can never love a man who frightens you," returned the violinist; "so I must conclude, Paulina, that you have no kind of affection for me. I must cease to see you; I must try if I can cease to care for you."

"You mistake me, Gustave——"

"Then why did you say I frighten you?"

"I was wrong, perhaps. I was thinking of my uncle, and his wild ideas."

"What ideas?"

"Why, his wish that I should marry a rich man."

"But I shall not be always poor, Paulina; promise me you will wait a little time for me." He seized her hand as he spoke.

"I think I may promise that, Gustave, for you may be sure I will never consent to marry against my will."

"In three years," continued the young man, "my position will be assured, and we shall both be still quite young; that would be a good time to arrange a marriage——"

At this moment Lanfredi awoke; the last words seem to have fallen with some effect upon his ears.

"Who talks of marriage?" he asked, sitting bolt upright in his arm-chair.

"I do, my dear master," said Gustave, taken by surprise, but not losing his self-possession. "I was telling Mademoiselle Paulina of some of my projects——"

"And you may keep them to yourself," interrupted his master. "Do not tell me *you* think of marrying. It is absurd—pure folly!"

"My dear sir," said Gustave, "I have always believed that such a subject entered the thoughts of every sensible man."

"But are *you* a sensible man? You are an artiste!"

"Dear master, do listen to a word——"

"You are a violinist, I repeat, and the senses of a violinist are not like those of other people. Marriage! Good heavens! you do not know what it is! Fancy having a woman dangling on your arm —and all the consequences: an establishment to keep up, visits to make, friends to entertain, children that run all over the house, squalling, quarrelling, tearing your music, breaking your instruments —how could you ever compose anything in such a row? Marriage for an artiste is life in the infernal regions—it is impossible!"

"Monsieur Lanfredi," said Gustave mildly, "is it possible to say such dreadful things of a state of life you confess to have had no experience of?"

"Experience! No, thank Heaven, I have never had such an experience! And you may be sure that if ever any other love than that of art had made me fool enough to give way to temptation, I might, that same day, have tied a brick to my violin and sunk it in the river!"

Paulina threw a glance at Gustave, as much as to say, "That is enough." The moment was not propitious for further conversation, and Gustave felt that two victories in one evening was rather more than he had any right to expect.

· · · · · ·

On leaving Lanfredi's house after the dinner party and concert, Maurice Stein returned home with feelings which it would be difficult to describe. The cool air of the evening did not calm down his exasperation. He flung himself on his bed, but his highly feverish state allowed of no repose. Project after project revolved in his mind, and it was many hours before sleep closed his weary eyelids. The next morning he awoke rather late; his mind was more tranquil. He began to reflect. At first he was rather ashamed of his conduct at the little concert. Was it not possible, he thought, that after all he might be mistaken? Was it not natural for two young persons to give evidence of sympathy over a piece of music, without love being necessarily mixed up in it?

He went to the violin class next day with a firm step, and a calm expression on his features. On his return in the afternoon he met Gustave coming from a rehearsal at the Opera, and about to take his usual frugal repast at a restaurant. There was a certain coldness in this meeting. Though Maurice was the first to offer his hand, the grasp was not of that warm character which for years past they had been accustomed to.

This state of things prevailed for about two

months, when Maurice Stein's health began to give way. His impetuous nature could not brook the isolation in which he found himself. His sleepless nights were passed in restless anxiety.

It happened one day that Gustave had gone to superintend the repairing of an old violin, and was absent for many hours. Maurice met Paulina in the music room, and begged her to accompany him in a new solo he was anxious to try. Lanfredi also urged his niece to comply, and left the young couple for a time entirely to themselves. At the conclusion of the piece Maurice thanked her most warmly, and said—

"Ah! Mademoiselle, if I could always find such a pianist as you, how happy I should be!"

"But," said Paulina, "there are many, I am sure, that would do far more justice to you——"

"It would make my fortune," interrupted Maurice, with such a searching glance of his ardent dark eyes that Paulina felt quite abashed as she closed the music and handed it to him. "Can I not hope," he continued, "that some day you will try to have a little esteem for me?"

"Monsieur Stein," said Paulina, evidently troubled, "I have the greatest esteem for you already. Are you not my uncle's finest pupil? Are you not the very best violinist in Paris?"

"It is not that I mean," said Maurice, with a sigh. "Will you not believe me when I say that I hope to gain your affection for myself alone? Do you think you could ever love me, Paulina?"

"Monsieur Stein, you must not talk to me in that manner," said the young girl, with visible emotion on her lovely features, "and I must not reply to such questions."

So saying she fled to her uncle's room, leaving Maurice in a state of bewilderment and despondency. The blow was too much for his excitable nature. A sleepless night and violent headache kept him in bed next day; and for a whole month he was unable to leave his room.

When he returned to the violin class he looked poorly, and he played badly. His altered appearance attracted the attention of Lanfredi. As the pupils were retiring he called Maurice back to him. "Come here, my boy," he said; "I have something serious to communicate to you."

Maurice approached him.

"My good friend," continued Lanfredi, "I am not blind, and I am not deaf. You look ill, and you are falling off in your playing. I noticed that the G sharp at the commencement of the Sixth Concerto was as flat as flat could be, and the passage of double notes that follow was thin, poor, and false, as if a child of ten had drawn the bow! Now, what is the matter?"

"I declare to you, my dear master——"

"Now, what do you declare, sir?" interrupted

Lanfredi. "Look at yourself in that mirror—you have a most wretched appearance. You are leading too fast a life, my young friend. Out with it, sir, tell me—is it gambling? is it late hours and bad companions? are you in debt? Make a clean breast of it, my child, and if I cannot do something to put a stop to it, I shall be much astonished."

The young man raised himself to his full height.

"You are quite mistaken, my master," he replied calmly. "I live a most quiet life; I hate gambling; I have no bad companions; and I have no debts."

"What can it be, then? Is it possible, my poor child, that unsatisfied ambition is wearing away your substance. All great artistes have had their hours of disappointment. Do not mind it, my dear young fellow——"

"No, my master, that is not it either."

"Oh! well, then, I give it up. I never was good at finding out an enigma."

"The enigma would not be difficult, perhaps, to any one else; but, Monsieur Lanfredi, you have often set your mind against marriage, and may be you have never known the power of love——"

"What!" ejaculated Lanfredi, "you are in love! you young idiot!" and he was, doubtless, about to deliver to Maurice some such oration as that bestowed on Gustave. But after a moment's reflection he shook his head and said—

"I really believe that you are incurable, my poor

young friend; and if so, you are dead as far as music is concerned. But though I may despair of seeing you a glorious artiste, I may yet save you as a man. Tell me everything; tell me what I can do to help you."

"You can do much," replied the young man; "you can do everything."

"Ah, gracious heavens! can it be——"

Before he could utter the name of Paulina, Maurice had nodded assent to the unfinished question.

"Dear me! dear me!" exclaimed the old professor, passing his hand over his forehead, as if to assure himself he was not dreaming, "this is most singular."

And then, after a few moments of silence, he turned abruptly to the young violinist and said—

"Without speaking of your mother's fortune, you have, I believe, some private means?"

"About 2000 francs a year."

"Well, I could give Paulina 20,000 on her marriage, and that would yield you another 1000 francs a year. You would not be rich, but it would enable you to wait for better things."

Then another long silence ensued, after which Lanfredi said—

"But I should not like to part with my niece; I have got accustomed to her society, and, I must say, I should regret to see her run away with——"

"I would never run away with her," interrupted

Maurice. "Heaven forbid that such an idea should ever enter my mind!"

"What!" said his master, "if you married Paulina, you would never leave the violin school? I should be allowed to live with you both as long as I could draw a breath? Well, I shall certainly insist upon that being in the contract."

The young man threw himself into his old professor's arms, sobbing aloud, and muttering the words, "Uncle! father!"

"And I should always be your *master*, you young jackanapes. I would give you a month for your honeymoon, and after that, mark me, you should again become a violinist!"

After that interview Maurice Stein was frantic with joy. His appearance changed rapidly for the better, and his excited manners astonished some of the other pupils. The next time he happened to see Gustave, he ran to meet him, clasped him in his arms, saying he felt quite ashamed of himself.

"I have been very unkind to you, Gustave, but you will forgive me; I feel sure you will."

"All is forgiven, all is forgotten," replied Gustave Lafont.

"Ah! if you only knew what I have suffered these last few months," continued Maurice. "My mind was upset, I was all but lost. But, thank Heaven, now all is well; happiness has come to me at last. What fate on earth could any man dread with such a friend as you, and such a wife as Paulina?"

"Paulina!" exclaimed the other, perfectly stupefied.

"My friend," continued Maurice, carried away by his enthusiasm, and not noticing the exclamation, "congratulate me. I have just obtained her uncle's consent."

Gustave fell back upon a chair and hid his face in his hands. "Oh! what misfortune has befallen me!" he exclaimed; "what have I done to deserve this?"

Then at last Maurice came to his senses. "What could I have been thinking of?" he muttered, as he went out. "How did I come to tell this to Gustave? He must, of course, be my rival; we can *never* be friends!"

. . . . . .

Paulina was just the age at which the charms of women are most attractive. It would have been impossible to find a more exquisite face, a more elegant figure, such speaking eyes, such an enchanting smile. Her dark auburn hair, which fell in luxuriant clusters over her forehead and shoulders, set off the rich southern tint of her beautiful features, and her short-skirted dress displayed the prettiest feet and ankles imaginable. Her disposition was gay and amiable; her quick, elastic step and every movement were characteristic of the happiest time of youth. Nature had smiled upon her, and she returned that smile tenfold. Her plighted troth to Gustave had opened up a new vista in Paulina's life, and had, if possible, increased her happiness. Her thoughts were now equally divided between his welfare and her uncle's comfort.

After his singular interview with Maurice, the worthy professor went straight to his niece's room. He entered smiling, and with outspread arms.

"Paulina," he cried, "come and embrace me."

"With all my heart, dearest uncle," said his charming niece, rushing up to him and kissing him on both cheeks.

"And thank me," he added, "for bringing you a piece of good news."

"Good news, uncle!"

"Yes—the poor fellow was in a state to make one's heart break. . . . I am not a man of flint, you know, and from one question to another we never know where it all leads to. . . . Well, at any rate, I have given my consent."

"Consent to what?" asked Paulina, whilst an expression of vivid curiosity spread over her lovely features.

"Now, now! Pretend to be ignorant of it all, of course, you sly little girl. As if you did not know as much as I do, and perhaps more! However, I must warn you that I have settled the conditions; there is to be no separation. This house is quite large enough for two establishments; nothing will be changed, except that instead of a pupil I shall have a nephew, and instead of your being called Mademoiselle you will be called Madame."

Paulina could scarcely contain herself for joy. Two more ardent kisses were promptly impressed upon her old uncle's cheeks.

"My dearest uncle," she said, as she grasped his dry, sinewy hands, "if you only knew how much I love you! But still, I cannot realise it—has he really had the courage to ask your consent personally?"

"Thank you for the compliment, my dear niece," said Lanfredi; "do I look like a man that any of my violin pupils could be afraid of?"

"Only fancy!" said Paulina, "after the sermon about marriage that you gave him that Sunday evening—I should never have believed it possible!"

"What is all this gibberish you are talking? You say I gave Maurice a sermon on marriage?"

"No, dear uncle, not Monsieur Stein, but Monsieur Gustave."

"You must be silly, my dear girl—or perhaps I am. What has Gustave got to do with this affair?"

Paulina fixed her large, dark eyes upon his; the flush of excitement left her cheeks, and her face took a pale, anxious expression, which quite astonished Lanfredi.

"Gracious Heaven, uncle!" she exclaimed, "who is it you want me to marry?"

"Why, Maurice, of course, to whom I have just given my consent."

"But that is perfectly frightful!" cried his niece. "I do not love Monsieur Stein—I cannot be his wife—I am betrothed to another!" and tears now rolled down the pale cheeks of Paulina. They were the first tears Lanfredi had ever seen shed by her, and his heart was melted in a moment.

"And that other—is Gustave, I suppose," he said, after a pause.

"Dearest uncle," said Paulina, placing her arm coyly round his waist, "just consider what a serious thing this is——"

"It is indeed," interrupted her uncle; "and pray how am I to get out of this difficulty—how can I break my word to Maurice?"

"Oh, my good little uncle, you will simply tell him that I have given my word to Monsieur Gustave."

"That is just what I will *not* do," put in Lanfredi, "for Gustave cannot, and shall not, be your husband."

"What obstacle might there be, uncle?" inquired Paulina calmly.

"What obstacle? Well, if you could live on love and cold water, as young people of your age often think they can, it would be all right; but with the experience gained at my age, I know it would be all wrong. To speak plainly, Paulina, I cannot give you very much, and Gustave has not got a penny."

"But he has talent——"

"Yes, decided talent, but the keen blasts of misery would soon destroy it."

A great deal more was said on this occasion than we have space to report. Lanfredi loved his niece too well to permit her to fall into the misfortune of marrying a man who could not support her.

"The deuce take youth and love!" he exclaimed, as he rushed from the room, lest he should again see his niece burst into tears, which was more than his sensitive nerves could bear.

The veteran violinist walked about a good while in the streets of Paris after that trying interview, endeavouring to discover, if possible, some solution to the difficult problem before him. On his return he sent word to Maurice to come and dine at the Violin School, at which the young musician was extremely delighted.

When dinner time came, it was found that Paulina could not be present. She complained of headache, and desired to pass the evening alone in her own room. Maurice was much disappointed at this; but Gustave did not appear displeased.

During the repast the conversation was slight and ordinary; but when the cigars were lighted, and dessert was on the table, it took a most interesting turn.

"My dear Maurice," said Lanfredi, "I have been rather too prompt in coming to conclusions regarding Paulina. You need not frown; I shall not withdraw what I have said to you and to her. But I have found that she is attached to Gustave, who has as much affection for her as you have, and I find myself in presence of two claimants instead of one. Now, my dear children, you know I am equally fond of you both, and I do not wish to do any injustice to either; so I have come to the following decision. In Paris to-day I learnt that Severini, who is getting old, is giving up his post as leading violin at the Opera. The position is to be offered for competition. Go, both of you, and get yourselves inscribed for this competition, which is to begin next week, and whichever comes out victorious shall have the hand of my niece. That is my ultimatum."

We cannot say precisely what Paulina would have thought of her uncle's conduct on this occasion. It made a very different impression upon each of the two violinists: to Gustave it appeared like a harbour of refuge; but to Maurice it seemed almost equivalent to shipwreck in the open ocean. He fell back in his chair without uttering a word. After a little while, however, he recovered himself, and both young men consented to compete.

The position was well worth trying for. Independently of the prize that the worthy old professor attached to it, it represented about 4000 francs a year, an income not to be despised in those days by the very foremost of violin players and professors of harmony.

. . . . . .

Maurice Stein rushed home, informed his mother of what had occurred, seized his violin, which for the last few months he had very much neglected, and worked away far into the night. The next morning he fled to the office of the Opera House to inscribe his name among the competitors. Gustave Lafont also inscribed his name the same morning.

The competitors were rather numerous, including some of the best musicians in Paris, and not a few from the provinces. Many of the newspapers had made known what was going to happen, and the event was talked about in the cafés and in musical circles as likely to prove one of the most exciting episodes of the season.

In a state of feverish frenzy, Maurice had no sooner returned home than he again took up his violin, and laboured hard to make up for lost time. But the more he strove, the more dissatisfied he became. Bodily fatigue and mental anguish combined to deter him from succeeding in his efforts. So true is it that no musical work is of any avail

THE VIOLIN SCHOOL AT NEUILLY 215

when done under the pressure of fatigue and excitement.

In less than three days, with rage and disgust, he flung down his violin, inwardly vowing that he would relinquish the task. But, for all that, he would not give up Paulina.

After revolving several projects in his mind, he came to the determination of provoking his rival to mortal combat. He never thought of his good, kind mother; maddened by his utterly selfish desires, he decided to compel Gustave to give up all claim to the hand of Lanfredi's niece, to quarrel with him, insult him, strike him, and meet him next day on the duelling ground. It never occurred to him what Paulina would think of the man who should kill her friend in a duel. He was simply blind with rage, intoxicated with jealousy, insane with selfishness and false pride.

Lanfredi, who in former days had travelled over the whole of Europe with no other companion than his Amati violin, who had known the time when his hotel-keeper had to give him a night's board and lodging in exchange for a little display of his talent, who had passed through the disappointments and struggles inherent to a wandering artiste's life, and had come out of all this unscathed, unsullied, and content with his lot, was not a man likely to fail in ensuring the happiness of his much-loved niece under these critical circumstances. He doted upon her; and he loved his two favourite pupils also. It was certainly a difficult thing to satisfy them all, and himself at the same time.

His little stratagem regarding the competition had occurred to him as one means of solving the problem. He knew that Paulina had accepted Gustave; he knew the character of the latter, and that of Maurice; and it was almost certain that if the appointment were won by either of his pupils, it would be the cool-headed Gustave that would gain the day, that the very impetuous nature of Maurice would carry him too far.

But there was another alternative : it might happen that neither of them would be chosen for the highly responsible and lucrative post. They were both very young men, and that fact alone would prove a great obstacle in so important a competition. It was, indeed, a post which required a greater knowledge of music than either Gustave or Maurice possessed. It would be given, of course, to some man who was intimately acquainted with all the works of the modern composers as well as those of bygone times.

Nevertheless there is a good old adage that says, " Nothing venture, nothing win," and Gustave Lafont worked diligently and carefully, buoyed up by the thoughts of his dear Paulina, until the critical time fixed for the great competition.

THE VIOLIN SCHOOL AT NEUILLY 217

Meanwhile Maurice took steps to carry out his diabolical plans.

. . . .

It was a dull morning early in November when Maurice Stein came down to breakfast with his mother.

"You look ill, my dear son," said Madame Stein; "have you not slept well?"

"No, mother, I have not slept at all; but I shall soon be better—only my head aches, and that, perhaps, makes me look ill."

"Now, Maurice," said his mother, "you must not give way any longer to this folly. Paulina Lanfredi is not worth all these exertions and anxieties. Think how many thousands of young girls, quite as beautiful and as talented, are to be found in the world—in Paris alone."

"No, mother," interrupted Maurice, "there is not one like her. You do not know her. But I have given up all idea of competing for the leadership at the Opera."

"You are right, my boy; I am glad of it."

"Yes; I shall compete with Gustave himself."

"What do you mean, Maurice?"

"Why, mother, I shall do what all other gentlemen do in similar circumstances—I shall challenge him, and fight him."

"Heaven forbid!" exclaimed his mother. "Only fancy, if this affair should lead you to a criminal action, Maurice! Do you think Paulina Lanfredi would not abhor any man who could act in such a manner? Then, suppose he killed you," continued Madame Stein, as tears rose to her eyes, "you do not think of me—what should I do?"

"My dear mother," said Maurice, "there is a kind Providence that protects those who are in the right—that guides our weapons in the duel——"

"No, Maurice," said Madame Stein, interrupting her son in a piece of bad philosophy, "no, a thousand times no! Even supposing you were in the right, the duel is the outcome of man's liberty. We have power over good and evil. Providence has given us this liberty, and if we abuse it, the sin falls upon our own heads."

Then, after a few moments of silence, the good woman added—

"Take my advice, Maurice, whilst there is yet time. Let us quit Paris, where we have few friends; let us travel together, and seek a new life. You are now an artiste, and there is nothing to prevent your following in the footsteps of Lanfredi, and becoming, perhaps, even more successful."

Maurice placed his elbows on the table, covered his face with his hands, and remained for some time in deep reflection. When the breakfast was ended, he rose and warmly embraced his mother without saying a word. He then took up his instrument and left the house.

THE VIOLIN SCHOOL AT NEUILLY 219

He went straight to the Violin School, walking briskly to arrive in good time. He opened the little garden gate, and stood for a moment in the hall.

He was still brooding over his determination to bring an insult upon Gustave when the luscious tones of a fine violin caught his ear. It was a slow, exquisite melody which caused his heart to throb. For the second time since the memorable evening when Gustave and he swore a lifelong friendship, he heard that lovely air of the *Gazza Ladra*.

Tears rose in his eyes, and he stood motionless, scarcely daring to draw his breath, as the sublime melody flowed through the house and riveted him to the spot. At last it ceased.

"No!" he muttered to himself, "mother is right. Adieu, Paulina! Adieu, Lanfredi! Adieu, Gustave!" and he rushed from the hall into the dismal November atmosphere.

"There is at least one woman in the world who cares for me," he thought, "and I will confide in her."

. . . . . .

Maurice was never more seen in Paris. Gustave came out of the competition with tolerable credit, but he did not come out victorious. A gentleman old enough to be his father, and whose name was quite celebrated in the musical world, was chosen on this occasion.

"Well," said Lanfredi, "you have done your

best, my boy; I could not expect more; and you had a very good display of points."

For some time Gustave Lafont continued his engagement in the orchestra of the Opera, but after having married Paulina, at the little Church of St. Brie, he gave it up, and succeeded Lanfredi as the director of the Violin School at Neuilly, which for a long time enjoyed considerable notoriety.

Several years afterwards the newspapers spoke frequently of a most distinguished violinist who was creating quite a *furore* in Austria, Germany, and Russia. His name was Maurice Stein, and they spoke of him as a German artiste. But it was soon found out that he was a pupil of the great Lanfredi.

Like his worthy master he never married, but he left, in his turn, two very distinguished pupils in the persons of Ernst and Vieuxtemps, who came to him for finishing lessons in Vienna.

If you wish to know, dear reader, how Maurice Stein played, look at Vieuxtemps' *Fantaisie Caprice*, which that celebrated violinist composed after those lessons in Vienna.

XVII

THE "SOUL" OF THE VIOLIN, OR THE SECRET OF THE SOUND-POST

THERE is a little piece of wood which stands upright between the table and the back of the violin, just behind the right foot of the bridge. The English call it the "sound-post," but the French have termed it *l'âme du violon*—"the soul of the violin." And it well deserves the latter denomination, for everything seems to depend upon it. Of the many separate pieces of wood of which a violin is composed, this is certainly the most important. Indeed, without it, the finest instrument is absolutely worthless.

It consists of a small, solid, cylindrical piece of old, well-seasoned, sound pine wood weighing 8 to 10 grains, and it is placed in its position, after the violin is made, by means of a curved steel instrument, called a "sound-post setter," which is sold in the shops for a shilling or two.

It is set whilst the violin is unstrung, or, at least, when the strings are all quite slack, and the bridge down. As soon as it is fixed in *its proper position*, the strings are tightened a little, and the bridge properly adjusted; then, after a little time has elapsed, the strings are gradually raised to concert pitch.[1]

I have italicised the words "its proper position," for upon this depends to a very great extent the quality of tone that the violin will produce.

The greatest violinists and the greatest instrument makers have had their utmost ingenuity turned to this tiny piece of wood, and many a violin is "made or marred" according to the attention which has been bestowed upon it.

The violinist and composer, Louis Spohr, in his well-known "Violin School," devotes some important remarks to the sound-post; and almost all writers who have treated of stringed instruments played with a bow, have duly appreciated the importance of this little bit of wood. Still, few persons appear to be aware how very much depends upon it, and the instructions that have been given hitherto regarding it are not altogether satisfactory. I have therefore thought it would prove interesting and profitable to give the results of my own experience on this subject, to which for many years past I have devoted a great deal of attention.

If any one would like to prove how much is due to this little cylinder of solid wood, let him take it

---

[1] The pitch of the Royal Italian Opera, *not* "Philharmonic pitch."

THE "SOUL" OF THE VIOLIN 223

out of the instrument, and then draw the bow over the strings. He will find that he can now produce only a very weak sound, and a sound that, in most cases, is of an atrocious quality. Hence the English term "sound-post" is not so inappropriate; for without it there is no sound worth speaking of, and the quality of sound a violin will produce depends almost entirely on the manner in which this said sound-post is placed in the instrument.

After telling the student what kind of violin he should seek to obtain for solo-playing, the great Spohr goes on to say that he should next devote attention to the position of the sound-post. He tells us what a difficult thing this is to carry out properly, and how much depends upon it. Still, it is scarcely to be recommended to the young musician who may happen to possess a really valuable instrument; indeed, it is not difficult to permanently injure a violin by moving the sound-post about too often, and for this purpose it is best to engage the services of a competent violin-maker, unless considerable experience has been acquired by operating upon instruments of slight value.

What I may term the *secret of the sound-post* was discovered by a gentleman in London many years ago, and with considerable advantage to himself. It was at the time I had the honour of acting for four years as president and violin solo to the Bohemian Orchestral Society. When we gave concerts we occasionally had to engage the service of a contra-bassist and a leader of the second violins. The latter office was more than once filled by an admirable musician, a Mr. B., a man of some fifty years of age, whose time was chiefly devoted to orchestral music, and who was one of the steadiest leaders it was possible to meet with. Our second violins were really admirable under his careful guidance. But besides his great knowledg of music and his powers as a player, Mr. B. was well acquainted with the construction of the violin ; and one of his hobbies was to "pick up," in out-of-the-way places, some cheap instrument, and by assiduous care to convert it into a very valuable violin.

More than once he was offered large sums fo violins that only cost him a pound or two ; but he was so proud of them when he had made them perfect, that it was only under the greatest pressure that he could be induced to part with them.

He never let me know his secret, but I discovered it some years afterwards ; and I now know that it consisted chiefly in paying great attention to the *fitting* and *position* of the sound-post—the "soul of the violin."

Now let us go a little deeper into this important subject. I will suppose we are dealing with a violin that is tolerably well made ; not one of those wretched instruments that are sold for a few shillings,

THE "SOUL" OF THE VIOLIN

but a violin whose outline and general appearance lead us to believe that it is made of good wood, of the proper thicknesses; say, an instrument of a certain age, that would be sold for £5 or £10 by a dealer. In many such cases, if proper attention be given to the sound-post, it will be quite possible to make this instrument almost equal to a fine Tyrolean or Cremona violin worth, as times go, hundreds of guineas, provided that it has not a strong nasal quality of tone. For the latter depends upon faulty outline and faulty thicknesses, and is probably quite incurable. But as this bad quality can be detected the moment the bow is passed over the strings, no violin possessing it would be likely to repay our trouble. Nevertheless, even in such a bad case as this, the sound-post may be made of such a quality, and placed in such a position, as to give a greater roundness or fulness to the tone. The first thing we have to consider is the quality of the wood and the thickness of the post. It must be cut from the best kind of red pine-wood, as old as possible, with straight fibres, without knots, and must be perfectly cylindrical and smooth.

It has been found that pine-wood which is old and sound may yet have different acoustic properties, as the old makers of violins knew so well. So much so, indeed, that (wood of such good sounding properties being difficult to obtain in their days) when a good piece of wood was found, any little blemishes it might have were carefully patched up. Thus in old Cremona and Tyrolean instruments of superior quality we sometimes meet with little square bits of wood that have been let into the table, which the workman has done rather than seek for another piece more perfect in appearance, but of less good acoustic properties.

This sounding quality is put in evidence by suspending the wood on a thin string and striking it with a stick; or by letting pieces of it, a few inches long and about half an inch broad, fall upon a hard slab, and noticing the quality of sound emitted. I have in my possession eight pieces of common deal of this size (such as is used for lighting fires), which have been cut of different weights, and when dropped, one after the other, on to a stone floor, they produce a perfect scale of one octave. In making this experiment it is easy to hear that some of the pieces produce more musical sounds than the others.

With regard to the exact thickness of the sound-post, it is not very material; for, on account of the limited width of the sound-holes of a violin, it is impossible to pass through them a cylinder of wood that is thicker than their opening at the widest part, *i.e.*, in the middle of the sound-hole. And this is almost exactly the thickness which is, perhaps, best suited to all instruments. But, for

THE "SOUL" OF THE VIOLIN 227

the last twenty years or so, some makers have been in the habit of using very narrow cylinders of wood—very thin sound-posts, and the reason of this is that they require less bevelling at the extremities in order to make them fit perfectly against the back and table of the violin. Others, with probably more reason, prefer a post as thick as can be introduced easily through the centre of the right sound-hole. A very thin post is apt to work a hollow place in the table, and is to be deprecated.

Now comes the most important consideration— the *exact position* which the sound-post should have in the body of the instrument.

Supposing the wood of which this little solid cylinder is constructed to be perfectly good, old, light, sonorous, free from blemish, and straight of fibre, perfectly cylindrical and smooth, with its upper and lower extremities slightly bevelled to enable it to fit exactly the slopes of the back and table, where is it to be placed in order to give the violin the finest quality of sound that it is capable of producing? That is the question I shall now endeavour to answer.

First I will quote a few words from a great authority on this subject, who says :—" The soundpost is made of choice fir with the fibres running straight through it lengthwise ; the older it is the better, provided it is sound, *i.e.*, not decayed, knotty, or blemished. It should be set when the instrument is unstrung, and should then be sufficiently tight to stand firm when the violin is shaken. It should be set in a line with the right foot of the bridge, and just so far behind as to leave about three-eighths of an inch between the front of the post and the back of the foot of the bridge. Weak violins, however, require it nearer to the bridge. Much discrimination is required in placing this little post, as on it the quantity and quality of tone mainly depend."

Of course a carelessly made violin, which has not the proper degree of thickness left in the wood in the central portion of the back and the table, or which has a bad outline or model, can never have a very fine tone; but should these requirements exist only to an imperfect extent, yet the proper placing of the sound-post will rectify this imperfection as much as possible.

It will be remarked that in the quotation we have just made, the position of the post is set down at "three-eighths of an inch" behind the right foot of the bridge. Spohr says "just behind," and others have said "a quarter of an inch."

An old and eminent London maker, whom I knew intimately for many years, asserted, as the result of his long experience, that there was *only one position for the sound-post*, and if the violin did not sound well with the post in that position, it would

THE "SOUL" OF THE VIOLIN

never sound well with it in any other; and that is, "just behind the right foot of the bridge." Now, although this applies to most violins, it must be regarded as an error; and it is an error which guides most of the makers and repairers of violins of the present day, both at home and abroad. With a few noted exceptions, they all act by routine, having in many cases no ear for music; and it is certainly much easier to do so than to labour for days, or even months, to discover, for any given instrument, which is the *best* place for the sound-post. It is, in fact, a matter of experiment, as will perhaps be gleaned from what has already been said. But there are certain rules which may serve to guide us in making this experiment.

If the violin is very weak, the post may be placed *as near as possible to the foot of the bridge*, without being right under it; and wherever it is placed it must be *perfectly perpendicular*—that is a very important point. If the violin is loud and coarse, the sound-post must be placed *farther back, away from the foot of the bridge*, but still in a straight line from the right foot of the latter. If the higher strings, E and A, are too loud, it may be shifted *very slightly towards the centre;* if the lower strings, D and G, are too loud, and the treble weak, it may be brought *slightly nearer to the right sound-hole*.

Loud and coarse violins are perhaps commoner than weak instruments, and fortunately they are easier to deal with than the latter; it is almost always possible, by taking the sound-post back, away from the bridge, in a straight line from the middle of the right foot, to cause them to give a fine, even, brilliant, and soft tone, equally powerful on all the strings, allowing the note to come out clearly with the most delicate touch of the bow, and enabling the performer to swell each note with the greatest ease. But to achieve this result perfectly would be to make a very ordinary instrument almost as good as the finest Cremona or Tyrolean violin.

When trying such experiments, some days should be allowed to elapse after setting the post in any given position, and stringing up the instrument to concert pitch, in order that it may be firmly settled in that position, and in order to repose the ear of the performer. In some cases the post must be placed very nearly three-quarters of an inch behind the right foot of the bridge, and in others it may be within an eighth of an inch of the bridge. So that, in spite of the fixed position given in instruction books such as the "Manuel du Luthier" and other works copied from this, *there is no absolutely fixed position;* a very little difference leads to very great results, and the best results can only be got by the most careful and persevering experiments. I was several years over a case of this sort; not that the post was changed

THE "SOUL" OF THE VIOLIN 231

every day or even every month, but perfect success was finally achieved.

In his valuable instructions to violinists, Spohr devotes much space to the position of the sound-post, as we have already remarked, but he omits a very important fact, namely, the exact length of this little, solid cylinder; and all the books which have copied Spohr's "School" also omit to give any information on this subject. How are we to ascertain the exact length that the post must have? For, of course, it varies according to the model, raised or flat, of the instrument.

Well, there is an ingenious method of ascertaining this length, which was discovered by some clever man whose name has not come down to us. Probably the little device dates back in history as far as the days of Gasparo da Salo, or Andrea Amati, in the sixteenth century. It consists in passing a knitting-pin, or a stiff piece of wire, through the top round of the right sound-hole, until it touches the back of the violin, pinching the wire firmly with the thumb and finger exactly at the surface of the table, and drawing it out; it will then show the exact length which the sound-post must have.

This measure must be taken with the greatest care, and the little cylinder of wood cut exactly to it; for an error of a twenty-fourth of an inch in length will prove of considerable consequence. If too long, it cannot be fixed at all (it cannot be made to stand upright); and if too short, it is quite useless, and will fall down, or cannot be placed in the proper position. Some slight allowance must be made for the bevelling at each extremity, especially when the violin is one of a high model.

The fibres of the sound-post, when fixed, should be across those of the table, at right angles with them. This is realised by fixing the point of the setter *between the fibres* in the proper place for this purpose, which is about a quarter-inch from the top, and taking care that the hole left when the setter is withdrawn faces the right-hand sound-hole. It is, however, a matter of minor importance.

XVIII

THE BRIDGE, THE STRINGS, AND THE BOW

HAVING now said all that I can with regard to the *secret of the sound-post*, I will add a few words, by way of supplement to this subject, to show how the qualities given to a violin by a good sound-post, properly fixed in the best possible position, may be enhanced by three other things—namely, an appropriate bridge, strings of a proper quality and thickness, and a good bow.

Next to the sound-post, the bridge exerts the greatest influence upon the quality of the tone of a violin, and we cannot be too careful in our choice of a bridge that is perfectly appropriate to the instrument. Bridges are of various weights, thickness, and quality of wood. Some are denser than others, and weigh more. If a violin is loud, it will require a dense, heavy bridge; if weak, it will require a bridge as light and thin as possible.

The fitting of a suitable bridge can rarely be properly achieved by the amateur; it is a matter which requires great experience, and should be confided to perfectly competent men, such as Chanot or Withers, who make it a kind of specialty, and receive instruments from all parts of the world for this purpose.

If a bridge is too dense, it may be rendered thinner by means of sand-paper; but if made too thin, it is apt to break suddenly when being placed, or even (as once happened to myself) by hard playing.

With regard to strings, they are far more perfect at present than they used to be twenty or thirty years ago. There is now great competition among the various manufacturers in Italy, France, and Germany. Generally speaking, thin strings yield the finest quality of tone, and are easier to play upon; whilst thick strings enhance the brilliancy at the expense of the tone. Some instruments will be well suited with strings of medium thickness; and it is well, when a player has once discovered which thickness of strings suits his instrument best, to always adhere to it. On purchasing the strings, the thickness is ascertained by means of a little brass gauge sold for the purpose; or the dealer will gauge them for the purchaser.

The great English bow-maker Tubbs once told me that "the bow is the lung of the violin," and he was quite right: it is to the violin what the lungs are to the singer, and a rough, heavy bow will often spoil the notes of the finest instruments.

Whilst the making of violins is an art which has

steadily deteriorated since the early part of the eighteenth century, that of bow-making has, on the contrary, improved; and though fastidious people even now will give large sums of money for a bow by Tourte, Dodd, Tubbs, Vuillaume, &c., that is rapidly becoming a thing of the past. It is true that I recently saw £25 paid for a bow by the old French maker Tourte, who himself charged large prices, because he had the habit of breaking over his knees any bow he made which did not satisfy his ambition, and charged accordingly for those he sold.

At the present time very excellent bows may be had, varying in price from half a guinea to three or four guineas. It is a matter for experiment; but, generally speaking, it will be found that a light bow is best suited for solo-playing.

It is now as easy a matter to procure a good bow as a bad violin; there is, nevertheless, a vast difference in the quality, smoothness, and power of tone as given by various bows, especially in the case of a fine, delicate instrument, and a solo-player cannot be too particular in his choice in this respect.

The more a violin is played upon, the easier its vibrations become, and this has often been put down as the cause of the superiority of old over new violins. But that is not all: I have met with old violins in Germany—upwards of a hundred years old—that were atrocious; and I have seen very modern violins that were just the contrary.

Age and constant playing can never give a fine quality of tone to a badly-made instrument which has not the proper model and proper thicknesses.

We have met with several professors who were never content with their violins, and were always ready to change them, or purchase a superior instrument if they saw their way to do so. I may mention in this respect my late friend Henri Vieuxtemps, one of the most accomplished violinists of modern times, who changed his instrument several times as his position in the musical world improved, playing latterly upon a very fine violin by Storioni, and finally upon an expensive Joseph Guarnerius.

Ole Bull also began, as we have seen, with an old violin of unknown origin, given to him by his uncle; but later in life he attempted to make a violin for himself. Failing to get satisfaction in this respect, he purchased a Joseph Guarnerius, and finally a Nicolo Amati, supposed to be the finest Amati violin in the world. Others, however, like the well-known Charles Dancla, who possesses a French violin, by Gand of Paris, of very good quality, never change. This excellent artiste and composer has cherished his instrument throughout the whole of his long and honourable career. We have already related in a former chapter of this work how he tried a Stradivari violin that was lent to him for one of his concerts, and after playing

THE BRIDGE, STRINGS, AND BOW 237

upon it for ten days, decided to play upon his own instrument as usual. All who are interested in music should read Dancla's "Notes et Souvenirs," published at Paris in 1893. It is an excellent work to place in the hands of young musicians.[1]

Dancla was quite right; changing a violin is like changing the voice of a singer: you are no longer the same person with another violin.[2] Long years have accustomed you to all the peculiarities of your instrument; you can produce with it the utmost expression which it is capable of yielding, and, for however fine an instrument you may exchange it, a very long time must elapse to enable you to become as familiar with it as with the one you have had so many years.

If you have an inferior instrument upon which you can never hope to realise great things, every effort should be made to procure a better one as soon as possible. This is a more difficult matter than many might suppose. Putting aside expense, which is often a serious consideration, it is impossible even for an accomplished violinist to judge correctly of the real qualities of a violin until he has played upon it for a fortnight or three weeks. Often have I myself been deceived in this respect. A violin

[1] "Notes et Souvenirs, par Charles Dancla. Paris: Delamotte. 1893. Price 2 francs."

[2] De Bériot, Paganini, Sivori, and Joachim, as far as we know, have invariably performed upon the same violin with which they commenced their artistic career.

which on a first and second trial appeared a perfectly delicious instrument, turned out to be weak, and to possess no "carrying power"—that is to say, it was brilliant and luscious to the player, but not very audible at a distance. Another instrument that did not appear at all loud to the player was distinctly heard, in the softest passages, at the extremity of a large and crowded concert room. Another, again, which was loud and brilliant both to the player and to the audience, was decidedly unpleasant to many of the latter, from its peculiar quality of tone.

I could quote many such instances. If you are fortunate enough to possess a violin that has been proved to please the audience, though it may not give the player himself complete satisfaction, it should be cherished, and the violinist should strive to avoid playing on any other, and to become more and more accustomed to it. It is easy to play out of tune on a strange instrument, and that is the greatest of all faults.

This leads me, in conclusion, to say a few words upon the musical education of children. Now that the violin has become the most fashionable instrument, it must not be forgotten that it is also the most difficult to cultivate with success, and that years of arduous study are required to bring it to any degree of perfection.

Thousands of young girls have the violin thrust

THE BRIDGE, STRINGS, AND BOW 239

upon them by ambitious parents, because for the last twenty years it has become so much in vogue; and it is only in cases where there exists decided natural talent that anything approaching to satisfaction can possibly result. A correct ear is more essential in this case than in any other, and every child should first be taught to sing the solfeggio before he or she takes up the violin. It will thus be ascertained whether the ear is correct or not; and if not, the piano or the harmonium will prove more satisfactory, and save much valuable time, as well as disappointment.

We cannot too often recall to mind the words that the eminent Dr. Spohr addressed to his young students:—

"You have chosen the most difficult of all instruments, and one upon which it is only possible to make progress—or, indeed, to retain in after years what you have already acquired—by constant, daily practice. Your instrument is, however, that which most amply repays the labours of study; but not until the player has attained the full command of it."

XIX

PERSONAL RECOLLECTIONS OF HENRI VIEUXTEMPS.

HENRI VIEUXTEMPS, the successor to the celebrated De Bériot, from whom he had lessons, was one of the greatest performers on the violin that this century has known. He eventually succeeded De Bériot in the Conservatoire de Musique at Brussels; but owing to failing health, and little fondness for teaching, he soon gave up that honourable post, which was afterwards filled by Wieniawski, also one of the greatest violinists of modern times.

It was in the summer of 1852, at Ostend, that I made the acquaintance of Henri Vieuxtemps. His father tuned our piano in Brussels, where we then resided; a nice, quiet old gentleman with a very acute ear, who, by his regular attendance, kept our instrument in perfect tune, in spite of the hard thumping it often underwent from some of my fellow-students at the University.

As usual, we were spending the summer season at Ostend, and my chief objects of attention were to avoid being asked to play the violin at the

HENRI VIEUXTEMPS 241

Kursaal, and to keep out of the way, if possible, of the amiable Madame Dreyfuss (sister of Sir Julius Benedict), who would insist upon my playing *violino obbligato* to her songs. I was but nineteen years of age, and had no ambition to perform daily before strangers; my desire, on the contrary, was to roam far away over the sand-hills, with my excellent Belgian friend Macleod, who was a great naturalist, in quest of rare plants and mollusca. Nevertheless, in those days, as ever since, art and nature divided my time almost equally.

It was at the Kursaal at Ostend that I made my first public appearance as a violinist with Artot's *Romance* (sung in *Lucretia Borgia*), and the *Andante* to De Bériot's Second Concerto. About the same time I took, at very short notice, the leading violin part in a grand cathedral service at Ostend, at which the present King and Queen of the Belgians (then Duc and Duchesse de Brabant) were present. I frequently played *violino obbligato* to the songs of Madame Dreyfuss and Mademoiselle Frank, both exquisite singers. The latter was magnificent in contralto parts from Verdi's *Nabuco* and Donizetti's *Lucretia Borgia*. The former had a very pleasing mezzo-soprano; her singing was full of poetical refinement and expression; she had many admirers, none, perhaps, more ardent, nor more capable of judging, than Signor Riciardi, of the Italian Opera, who was an intimate friend of Henri Vieuxtemps.

Q

This well-known tenor had lately retired from the operatic stage, and was spending a little time at Ostend after a long engagement at Odessa. He had one of the sweetest and most expressive tenor voices I ever heard; but time and hard work had told upon it, and he was obliged to leave the Opera and resort to teaching. He was about to give a concert with Vieuxtemps when I met him one morning on the *digue*, as I was going for a dip in the briny waves.

"Phipson," he said, "I have asked my friend Vieuxtemps to hear you play. I am very anxious he should hear you—*vous avez quelque chose qui lui manque.*"

"My dear Signor Riciardi," I said, "you must be joking. I dare not play before Vieuxtemps."

"Oh, you need not fear," he rejoined; "he is a most kind, good-natured man. I am sure you will like him—and it is all settled; I was just now speaking to your parents at the Kursaal, and I am to bring Vieuxtemps to tea to your rooms to-morrow evening."

Well, Vieuxtemps and Riciardi came punctually at tea-time, and during that afternoon it had been arranged between my mother and myself that we should play the *Andante* to De Bériot's Second Concerto. I found the great violinist just what Riciardi had told me. He was a perfect gentleman in manners, though a little stiff, and a thoroughly

HENRI VIEUXTEMPS

kind-hearted man. I played the piece just mentioned, not without many "doubts and fears," before these eminent critics. When it was finished, and the last harmonic had floated away through the open windows, Vieuxtemps rose from his seat.

"*C'est bien! C'est bien!*" he exclaimed. "But do you not find it very difficult to produce the full tone on your violin?" he added, after a slight pause.

I replied that I did, and that it sometimes caused pain in the muscles of the neck.

"Ah! there is something wrong with the instrument," he said; "if you will bring it round to my lodgings in the morning, I will try to find out what is wanting."

I thanked him warmly for his kindness, and next morning took my violin to him. He kept it about a fortnight, and when I got it again it was certainly very much improved. But what it really wanted was a new bar. The old eighteenth-century bar was too weak, and it was only when Boulangier of London (then working for Withers) put in a new one, many years later, that the instrument became perfect.

Shortly after this Henri Vieuxtemps and Riciardi gave their concert at the Hôtel de Ville at Ostend. The room was well filled, and, of course, I was there. The two violinists Wieniawski and Kontski were present on this occasion among the audience, and Kontski afterwards gave a concert in the same rooms.

Madame Vieuxtemps, who was a splendid pianist, very often played her husband's accompaniments, but on this occasion she was not able to be present, and a gentleman, whose name I forget, supplied her place very creditably, and afterwards played a piano solo. Vieuxtemps played *Il Trillo del Diavolo* of Tartini, and his own *Fantaisie Caprice*. In the second part he gave a fantasia on Bellini's *Norma*, with a difficult variation on the fourth string. He was enthusiastically applauded. Riciardi sang a lovely romance by Massini, entitled *Une fleur pour réponse*, and the final tenor scene from Donizetti's *Lucia di Lammermoor*. That was the whole of the programme.

Vieuxtemps' execution was truly prodigious; his tone was very fine, and his intonation perfect. He had a splendid staccato. To me he appeared sometimes to lack expression in the cantabile passages; and in his variation on the fourth string almost every note rattled in a most disagreeable manner. He was extremely energetic on the fourth string. At that time he played on a fine violin by Storioni of Cremona, which he had himself arranged and made as perfect as possible. Later in life he parted with it and procured a Guarnerius del Gesu.

When we all returned to Brussels, Vieuxtemps came occasionally to tea, and to talk politics with my father, to whom he appeared much attached. It was then he proposed that I should travel with him as a pupil for five years, during which time, he declared, he could bring me out successfully as a professional violinist; but I was making very good progress in philosophy at the University, and it was finally decided that I should remain there. On one of these occasions our old friend Baron Von Rosenberg, of Dresden, an ardent amateur of music, who was then on a visit to Brussels, was present, and had a few warm words with Vieuxtemps, whom he declared he had never heard, and urgently desired to hear. At the moment this request was made Vieuxtemps had my violin in his hands, my mother was seated at the piano, and, with his usual good nature, he was about to comply with the old Baron's wishes, when the latter happened to let drop the word "Joachim." This was too much for Vieuxtemps.

"No," he said; "when I come out after a hard day's work for a little quiet chat with my excellent friend Mr. Phipson (alluding to my father), I do not expect to be asked to play, and to be told that, in spite of my numerous concerts in Dresden and Berlin, you have never heard me, but that you have heard Herr Joachim, with whom you would like to compare me, on a violin I am not accustomed to—*non! c'est un peu trop fort!*" and he quietly laid down the violin and let himself fall carelessly into an arm-chair.

The old Baron was very angry; but after a while

my father succeeded in pacifying them both, and Vieuxtemps promised that Von Rosenberg should hear him on another occasion; so they afterwards shook hands and parted pretty good friends.

Vieuxtemps' father was justly proud of his distinguished son. He one day made a present to my mother of a coloured lithographic portrait of the great artiste, at the age of eight, with his violin in his hands, taken shortly after his first public appearance. She has it still. It is a three-quarter picture, and the violin appears almost as big as the child. The latter has dark hair and eyes, and a most expressive, intelligent countenance; he is dressed in a grey blouse and white collar, with a leather belt round his waist.

When I first knew Henri Vieuxtemps he had already travelled in Europe, and had established his reputation as one of the greatest of violinists. In Belgium, when De Bériot had retired, he was considered to be the greatest in the world; for Sivori was then little known in that country, and Joachim alone seemed to vie with him.

I heard Vieuxtemps on several occasions besides that above mentioned, among others at a concert at the splendid room of the Grande Harmonie at Brussels, where he always had a very enthusiastic reception, and where Teresa Milanollo, whose acquaintance I also made about this time, more than once delighted her audiences.

When a concert by Henri Vieuxtemps was about to take place, we used to see in various parts of the city great posters on which the word

VIEUXTEMPS

was printed in enormous characters, each letter being more than a yard long. He appears to have been the first "star" violinist to adopt that fashion of announcing himself to the public. Of late years it has been copied *ad nauseam*, and quite small artistes announce themselves in big characters in our country towns. But from 1849 to 1859 this method of advertising was very exceptional, and usually produced a certain effect, because none but the greatest performers were so announced. If a comparatively unknown violinist had adopted such a measure, the result would have been very different; for it would have engendered ridicule, and nothing kills like ridicule in Belgium and France.

At his concerts Vieuxtemps appeared to revel in difficulties, and his playing was more or less of the Paganini school, but sobered down by the classical influence of De Bériot. As I have before said, he had a remarkably fine tone; at the slightest touch of his bow every fibre of the violin seemed to vibrate, and to produce the fullest and roundest tone of which the instrument was capable. His staccato and arpeggio were also the finest that could be heard. The only violinist I ever knew who perhaps equalled Vieuxtemps in the crispness and accuracy of his staccato was my worthy master Henri Standish, with whom it was almost a natural gift. I have heard it stated by the late Madame Jullien that Camillo Sivori had the finest staccato known; but as I never heard Sivori except in Paganini's music, where the stiff staccato is hardly ever used, I cannot judge of the value of this statement. Among living violinists Emile Sauret is remarkable in this respect. It is doubtless one of the most effective ornaments of violin playing, and well repays the drudgery of practice necessary to acquire it; but several distinguished violinists I could name have never succeeded in obtaining it to any extent.

Late in life Vieuxtemps suffered from paralysis, brought on, I believe, by overwork, as was the case with another eminent violinist whom I knew. He was on a visit to Algiers, a great invalid, and taking an airing with a friend in an open carriage, when a vile, drunken Arab threw a huge stone at him, which struck him on the back of his head and hastened his death. He was born in 1820 at Verviers, in Belgium, and died in 1881, leaving many fine compositions for the violin.

INDEX

AGE, its influence on the quality of a violin, 180, 235
Airs Variés, De Bériot's, 60, 61
Alard, his violin, 100; his Souvenirs des Pyrenées, 21
Albani, violin maker, 121
Alboni, Marietta, 90
Album Chanot, the, 15
Amateurs, distinguished, 34
Amati, Nicolo, his workshop, 103; his violins, 178, 182
Amber colour, 178
Andunsun, Thorgeir, the violinist, 147
Auber, violinist and composer, 64, 65

BALFE, as a violinist, 64; his songs, 66; his first dramatic composition, 70; his romantic career, 64-72
Baltzar, 34
Bannister, leader of the Royal violins, 33
Banti, Briggitta, 8, 166
Bassani, 3
Battista, Giovanni, 2
Beale, W., his work, 72
Bellini, his opera La Sonnambula, 196

Bériot, Charles de, 8, 17; appears in London before Paganini, 49; his career, 73; his two guiding principles, 75; interview with Viotti, 76; character of his performance, 81; pupils of, 87; compositions of, 88; at Bologna, 144; his violin, 237
Bériot, Ch. Vincent, 85
Betts, John, his Stradivari violin, 121
Bohemian Orchestral Society, the, xiii, 223
Bordogni, his celebrated studies, 70
Bow, celebrated makers of the, 235
Bow, choice of a, 234
Bow used in Mongolia, 113
Bric-à-brac hunters, 118
Bridge, its various qualities, 233
Bruni, 27, 31
Bull, Ole, and Norwegian poetry, 130; his family, 131, 132; his romantic career, 132-149; his violins, 236
Burmester, 130
Burney, Dr., 27
Byron, Lord, 185

INDEX

CALCAGNO, Signora, pupil of Paganini, 46
Campagnoli, 2, 9
Carnaval de Venise, Paganini's, 49; Ernst's, 62
Cassel, the town of, 150-159
Castrovillari of Padua, 3
Cerutis, the, of Cremona, 123
Cervetto, first instructor of Paganini, 51
Chanot, F. W., 15, 119, 233
Chanot, George, 105, 119; violin by, 178
Charles II., his band of violins, 33
Cherubini, flight from Paris, 12; as a violinist, 38; persecution of, by Napoleon, 43; his *Marguerite d'Anjou*, 41
Child violinist, the, 150
Children, musical education of, 238
Chimay, Prince de, 88
Choron, quotation from, 1
Ciandelli, pupil of Paganini, 46
Cimarosa, 14
Colbrand, Isabella, 145
Collector's craze, the, 98
Concerto, De Bériot's 2nd, 61
Concerts, origin of, in England, 35
Concerts Spirituels, 6, 27
Conservatoire de Musique, offshoot of the French Revolution, 43
Cooke, Tom, 67; anecdote of, 122
Corelli, 3, 4; extent of his scale, 54; his violin, 168
Costa, Giacomo, gives lessons to Paganini, 52

Cremona, the two Josephs of, 97; industries of, at the present day, 123; varnish of, 118, 142, 179
Cremona violins, patched or scraped, 117
Cremona violins, the craze for, 177
Cremona violins, present prices of, 100, 121
Cremona violin trade, the, 175

DALAYRAC, the composer, 22
Dancla, Ch., 119; his violin, 236; his book, 237
Der Freyschutz, Weber's opera, 69
Dodd, 235
Double harmonics of Paganini, 47; mode of executing, 60
Dragonetti, his double-bass, 168
Dreyfuss, Madame, 241
Duke, Richard, violin maker, 99

ELECTOR-STAINER violins, 122
English violin makers, 178
Ernst, 9; his *Carnaval de Venise*, 62
Experts, an anecdote, 108

FAYE, Countess de, and Ole Bull, 143
Fétis, 45
"Fiddle," signification of the word, 110
Forster, Dr., 122
Frankfort, music at, 159
Frascati's, Ole Bull at, 140
Frederick the Great, 165

GARAT, the tenor, 11, 14
Garcia, Maria Felicia (Malibran), xi, 82, 144

INDEX 251

Garcia, Pauline (Madame Viardot), 85
Gasparo da Salo, 79
Gaviniès, the violinist, 27
George, Henry Saint, 111
German violins sold as Cremonas, 128
Ghiretti, teacher of Paganini, 53
Gillott, his collection of violins, 118
Gilmour, music in Mongolia, 112
Giornovick, the violinist, 48
Gnecco gives instruction to Paganini, 52
Goethe, the poet, 159, 167, 168
Gounod, Ch., 2
Guadagnini, Lorenzo, 99
Guarneri, the violins of the, 100, 104
Guarneri, Giuseppe, del Gesu, 101, 102, 107
Guarneri, Giuseppe, figlio d'Andrea, 103
Guarneri, Andrea, 104
Guhr, the violinist of Frankfort, 47, 160

HANDEL, 3
Hérold, 15
Hiller, of Leipzig, 165
Horn, Ch. and C. F., 67, 68

INSTRUMENTS of old Cremona makers, 98 (*see also* Stradivari, Guarneri, Amati, Sebastian Kloz)
Italian criticism on Ole Bull, 144
Italian School, the, 1

JACOTOT's method, 75
Joachim, 116, 237, 245

KENNY, Life of Balfe, 72
Kloz, Sebastian, violins by, 117, 121, 129, 177, 180, 182
Kloz, Mathias, 178
Kontski, 243
Kreutzer, 48

LABELS, spurious, 118; obliteration of, 179
Lablache, Luigi, 83
Lady violinists, 162
Langlé, Marie and Ferdinand, 21
Larsen, Marcus, celebrated picture by, 132
Le Streggne, Paganini's composition of, 49, 50, 60
Lipinski, Ch., the violinist, 49
Locatelli, his violin music, 3, 47
London Gazette, 1672, extract from, 37
London violin dealers, 175
Lulli, Giovanni Battista, 32

MAGINI violin, De Bériot's, 79
Malibran, in London, 71; at Paris, 138; in Bologna, 144; her tomb in Brussels, 86 (*see* Garcia)
Mara, Madame, 166
Martinez, Isidora, her account of Ole Bull, 149
Masoni, 80
Maucotel, violin by, 119
Maurer, 136
Mayseder, 65
Mazzara, Count, befriends Balfe, 69
Mell, David, first English amateur violinist of note, 34
Merlan, Countess, 89
Mongolian fiddle, 112
Montebello, Duke of, 142

INDEX

Montegérault, Madame, and Viotti, 12
Mori, anecdote of, 18, 67
Mozart, his overture to *Il Flauto Magico*, 68; his violin, 117
Music of Ole Bull, 149
Music of Paganini, 54

NAPOLEON, persecution of Cherubini by, 43
Nardini, 40, 168
National Norwegian theatre, 147
Neil Gow, 147
Nilsson, Madame, 167, 168
Norman Neruda, 130
North, Roger, his "Memoirs of Music," 36
Norwegian musical festival, 130
Norwegian colony in America, 147

OPERA of Cassel, the, 136
Opera of Frankfort, 160
Oratorio concerts, 67
Orchestra, the, and the singer, 170
Orfila, 11
Ostend, music at, 241
Ottoboni, Cardinal, and Corelli, 5

PAER, the composer, teacher of Paganini, 53
Paganini, 3, 4, 8, 18, 25; his secret, 44; careful musical education, 45; double harmonics, 47; his three characteristic pieces, 49; spurious compositions attributed to him, 50; his mother's dream, 50; his father, 51; his first appearance, 52; his music, 54; tour in Lombardy, 57; as a solo player, 59; his sonatas, 62; anecdote of, 93; at Paris, 138
Pagin, the violinist, 27
Papini, Guido, 93; the compositions of, 2
Paradisi, 164
Pasta, Madame, 196
Philharmonic Society of Bologna, 145
Philharmonic Society of Christiania, 136
Phillips, Henry, his "Musical Reminiscences," 72
Poulsen, the Danish violinist, 133
Prume, his violin compositions, 54
Pugnani, 8, 15, 26; pupils of, 27

QUALITY of a violin, 105

RAFFAELE, 4
Ranz des Vaches, Viotti's, 20
Reade, Ch., 105, 176
Revolution, musicians in the, 41
Riciardi, the tenor, 241, 242
Robbrechts, the last pupil of Viotti, 76
Rode, Pierre, the celebrated violinist, 17
Rolla, Alessandro, teacher of Paganini, 53
Rondo de la Clochette, the, 49, 95
Rooke, the composer, 65
Rossini, a letter of, 15; his *Mosè in Egitto*, 16, 71; his *Guillaume Tell*, 16, 190; his two kinds of music, 58; his *Largo al factotum*, 70, 196, 197; his unaccompanied octet in *Matilda di Sabran*, 172; his *Gazza Ladra*, 191
Rossini, Madame, 145

INDEX 253

Royal violins, the, 32
Ruggeri, of Cremona, 178, 182

SACCHI, Frederico, 123
Saintou, 168
Salaries of singers and players, 170
Sarasate, 116
Scheinlein, violin maker, 177
Schmöhling, Herr, 150
Schmöhling, Elizabeth Gertrude, her first appearance in 1753 at the age of six years, 155; her reception at Vienna, 160 (*see* "Child violinist")
Schott brothers, their acquisition of Paganini's MSS., 50
Sembrich, Madame, 168
Shuttleworth, 37
Simon, violin maker, 177
Simonelli, Mateo, 3
Sinclair Lay, the, 131
Singelée, 74
Singelée, Mdlle., 168
Sivori, Camillo, pupil of Paganini, 46; a souvenir of, 90; at the St. Hubert Theatre, Brussels, 94; his violin, 91, 237, 248
Solo playing and orchestral playing, 172
Solo on one string at Cairo, 111
Somis, 26
Sonata del Diavolo, the, 6, 28
Sontag, Henrietta, 165
Sound-post, the secret of the, 221–232
Spohr, Louis, his birth, 49; and Ole Bull, 136, 150, 160; his remarks on the sound-post, 222; his address to young students, 239
Staccato bowing, 248

Stainer, Jacob, 120, 178, 180
Stamitz, J., 26
Standish, Henri, xii, 122, 248
Stradivari, his violins, 100, 121, 182
Stradiuarius, the, a dialogue, 124
Strings, choice of, 234

TARISIO, Luigi, 105
Tartini, 3, 4, 6, 27, 168
Terni, Giulio di, 6
Titiens, Mdlle., 74, 92
Tosti, compositions of, 2
Tourte, 235
Trial of violins, 237, 238
Tubbs on the bow, 234

VARNISH, the old Cremona, 118, 142, 179
Varnishers, the king of, 107
Ventriquattri Capricci, the, 56
Veracini, 7, 28
Verdi, his air of Manrico in *Il Trovatore*, 2
Versailles, scene at, 10
Viardot, M., 87
Vidocq, anecdote of the detective, 142
Vieuxtemps, his pieces, 55; personal recollections of, 240; concerts of, 247; his violins, 236; portrait of, 246
Viola d'amore, 2, 111
Violin, Paganini's, 62, 98; Sivori's, 91
Violin days of Balfe, 64
Violin playing, the art of, 55
Violin recital in Mongolia, 110
Violin school at Neuilly, the, 184
Violin school of Brussels, 73
Violin, a, of tinplate, 23

Violin, my first, viii
Violins, dealing in, 175
Violins, qualities of, 181
Violins, prices of, in the time of Stradivari, 126
Violins, adventure with a dealer in, 180
Violins by Sebastian Kloz, 117 (*see* Kloz)
Violins, old and new, 235
Violins of value, 100, 117
Violins of the Tyrol and Cremona, 99
Violins, characters of the Guarneri, 104
Violins made by Vuillaume, 91
Violinists, biographies of celebrated, 162

Violons du Roi, 33
Viotti, 3, 7; his début, 10; his writings, 14; pupils of, 17; a letter of, 28; flight to London, 43
Vismes, Prince de, 122

WAGNER, the music of, 2
Weber, 69
Wiele, the violinist, 136
Wieniawski, 54, 240, 243
Witches, The (*Le Stregghe*), 49, 60
Withers, 119, 234, 243

YOUSSOUPOFF, Prince, 89

ZAMPIERI, Marquis, 145

THE END

Printed by BALLANTYNE, HANSON & CO.
Edinburgh and London

www.ingramcontent.com/pod-product-compliance
Lightning Source LLC
Chambersburg PA
CBHW032007230426
43672CB00010B/2278